MATH IN PRACTICE

A GUIDE FOR
Administrators

MATH IN PRACTICE

A GUIDE FOR
Administrators

Susan O'Connell • John SanGiovanni

HEINEMANN
Portsmouth, NH

Heinemann

361 Hanover Street

Portsmouth, NH 03801–3912

www.heinemann.com

Offices and agents throughout the world

Library of Congress Cataloging-in-Publication Data

Names: O'Connell, Susan. | SanGiovanni, John.

Title: A guide for administrators / Susan O'Connell, John SanGiovanni.

Description: Portsmouth, NH : Heinemann, [2016] | Series: Math in practice |
    Includes bibliographical references.

Identifiers: LCCN 2016014981 | ISBN 9780325078236

Subjects: LCSH: Mathematics—Study and teaching (Elementary) | Elementary
    school administration.

Classification: LCC QA135.6 .O2855 2016 | DDC 372.7—dc23

LC record available at https://lccn.loc.gov/2016014981

Editor: Katherine Bryant

Production: Hilary Goff

Typesetter: Publishers' Design & Production Services, Inc.

Cover and interior designs: Suzanne Heiser

Manufacturing: Steve Bernier

Printed in the United States of America on acid-free paper

20   19   18   VP   2   3   4   5

To the passion and commitment of school leaders as they envision, design, and lead the way to innovative and effective elementary math programs

SO

To Kristen—Our math conversations make *me* better.

JS

Contents

Acknowledgments

The Math in Practice project has been a true collaborative effort. We are grateful to Heinemann for turning the project vision into a reality. We are also thankful for their attention to the often-forgotten role of the school and district leader in bringing about change in teaching. With our leaders informed and on board, change can happen.

Special thanks to the following administrators who welcomed us into their buildings: Joel Barnes (Blythe-Bower Elementary, Cleveland, TN), Michelle Carey (Grasonville Elementary, Grasonville, MD), Louise DeJesu (Hilltop Elementary, Glen Burnie, MD), Karen Soneira (Germantown Elementary, Annapolis, MD), and Troy Todd (Running Brook Elementary, Columbia, MD). Thanks to these math coaches and administrators who shared program information or artifacts to be included in the online resources: Cheryl Akers, Melissa Bishop, Jeanine Brizendine, Molly Caroland, Kathleen Carter, Bonnie Ennis, Shelley Fritz, Angie Goodwill, Kristen Mangus, Kimberly Quintyne, Renee Rewalt, Jennifer Stairs, and Joan Tellish.

Thanks also to the following teachers who agreed to be photographed during their professional learning: Kayla Caldwell, Hannah Fisher, Lindsay Gordon, Angie Hentz, Mary Murphy, Casey Prince, and Jon Skovira.

We are grateful to David Stirling for taking the amazing photos of students engaged in math tasks during our visit to Grasonville Elementary School. And thanks to Cheryl Akers and Joan Tellish for making cameo appearances in photos in this book.

Special thanks to our editor, Katherine Bryant, for her on-target suggestions and careful editing, but mostly for working side by-side with us to refine and enrich our words and enhance the final product. Thanks also to Hilary Goff, our production editor, for her tireless efforts during the production of this book and its related resources.

As always, thanks to our families for their constant encouragement and willingness to listen to our griping as we struggled to make deadlines. We owe you some uninterrupted time!

Introduction

For many years, we held a very narrow view of elementary mathematics, believing the goal was simply mastering basic facts and computations. If a student could memorize math facts and algorithms and find correct answers, he was considered proficient in mathematics. And yet, many of those students never understood what they were doing as they followed the series of memorized steps. Today, we have changed our views on what is truly important in the teaching of mathematics. We have a more comprehensive view of math proficiency. We expect our students to do math and also to understand the math they are doing, to be able to communicate that understanding, and to be able to apply skills to solve problems. We expect them to be mathematical thinkers, not just to follow a series of memorized procedures. We see elementary mathematics as providing a strong foundation of skills, concepts, and practices that are essential for our students' continued math explorations.

We have also questioned past beliefs about who can learn math. In the past, there was a sense that some people are "math people" while others are not, providing an excuse for why some students couldn't learn what was being taught. Today the expectation is that all elementary students can and should learn mathematics. And that it is our responsibility as teachers to find ways to help all of our students find success. Rather than teaching math in one way, regardless of our students' needs, we are challenged to alter our teaching so they are able to learn. Teaching mathematics has evolved from worksheets and drills to active involvement, investigations, hands-on experiences, and discussions. Our goal is to find instructional approaches that respect our students' different learning styles and acknowledge their varied levels of prior knowledge.

And certainly we are well aware of the disparate feelings people have about mathematics. Some adults look back at their classroom experiences with feelings of pride and accomplishment; others look back with feelings of frustration and embarrassment. Many students shut down in math classrooms at very early grades— many even in elementary school—feeling they could not do what was expected of them. These students grew into adults who stridently claim they don't know math and don't like math. Today, we recognize the importance of building confidence at the elementary level and nurturing a love of math.

We are challenged to rethink the teaching of mathematics to address a balance of thinking and computational skills, to motivate all students to be mathematical learners, to help students build confidence and feel capable in math endeavors, and to find ways to provide a strong math foundation for all of our students (see Figure I.1).

Figure I.1: Math classrooms should be engaging, thoughtful, and positive environments in which students make sense of math ideas.

What Constitutes an Outstanding Math Program?

Principles, standards, research, and position statements in recent years have helped us craft a new vision of elementary mathematics. As we consider the content we teach, the need to make math accessible to all students, and the need for research-driven instructional strategies, we restructure not only our personal views about math but the composition of the elementary math program.

GUIDING PRINCIPLES

In *Principles to Actions: Ensuring Mathematical Success for All* (NCTM, 2014), the National Council of Teachers of Mathematics (NCTM) identifies and describes six guiding principles for effective math programs.

- **Teaching and learning**—Outstanding mathematics programs are founded on good teaching.
- **Access and equity**—Outstanding mathematics programs are committed to ensuring that all students have the opportunity to learn mathematics.
- **Curriculum**—Outstanding mathematics programs provide a strong curriculum that develops important mathematics along coherent learning progressions and develops connections between math ideas and connections to the real world.
- **Tools and technology**—Outstanding mathematics programs integrate the use of mathematical tools and technology as essential resources to help students understand, communicate, and reason about math.
- **Assessment**—Outstanding mathematics programs ensure that assessment is an integral part of instruction and that it is used to make instructional decisions and program improvement.
- **Professionalism**—Outstanding mathematics programs have a culture of professionalism in which all stakeholders share the responsibility of making learning happen.

As leaders, these principles can and should guide our actions and decisions about our mathematics programs. They remind us to continually consider questions like the following:

Are we focusing on the learning of all of our students?

Are we providing solid progressions to support students' learning?

Are we using tools and technology to maximize our students' learning?

Are we continually assessing our students' progress and making adjustments to instruction based on what we see?

Are we constantly looking for new ways to refine and enhance our teaching to maximize our students' learning?

Are we instilling in our students a belief that they can do math?

WHAT CHANGES NEED TO BE MADE?

Our challenge is to determine what changes need to be made in order to better align our schools and districts with this new vision of elementary mathematics. Each school or district is in a different place in this transition, from past practices and beliefs to a new vision. For some, the transition is already happening, and the goal is to maintain the momentum and guide the change, while for others the goal may be to get the transition started.

See Math in Practice: A Guide for Teachers, pages 1–12.

A major component of this transition is examining our own attitudes and practices about teaching mathematics and assisting teachers in examining theirs. The Introduction to *Math in Practice: A Guide for Teachers* can help you, and the teachers you work with, think through this process, but here are some key aspects to consider.

What should we be teaching?

We have already touched briefly on the changes we want to see in math teaching and learning. Our expanded view of our math goals includes attention to the development of concepts, procedures, strategies, reasoning, and dispositions. In *Adding It Up* (National Research Council 2001), five critical strands of math proficiency were highlighted:

- conceptual knowledge—the understanding of math concepts and operations
- procedural fluency—the ability to fluently and accurately carry out math procedures
- strategic competence—the ability to represent and solve math problems
- adaptive reasoning—the ability to reason logically and justify and explain that thinking
- productive disposition—the ability to see math as making sense and as useful, as well as the confidence to believe that it is doable.

We recognize that the teaching of mathematics is about building our students' skills and understandings in all five of these interrelated strands.

Who can learn math?

As we said earlier, many people believe they are not "math people." This attitude often stems from experiences early in their math education. Too often, we think of math as something that is only for experts, or a special few, where in fact it is a rich and valuable subject that can and should be accessible to everyone. The belief that only some people can succeed at mathematics impacts equity in our programs and promotes achievement gaps within our students.

If we truly believe that all people can and should learn mathematics at a deep level, our role as teachers changes to include attention to varied learning formats to meet all students' needs, reliance on formative assessment to determine students' needs, and a focus on identifying effective strategies for reteaching and intervention. We must shift our focus to the learner rather than simply disseminate information.

What should a math classroom look and sound like?

For many of us, a math classroom was a silent place, or a place where only the teacher's voice was heard. Students sat in rows completing worksheets. "Eyes on your own paper!" was the constant cry. But is that what we believe a math classroom should look and sound like now?

Today we believe that proficiency in mathematics involves more than just getting the right answer to a computation. Standards like the Common Core Standards for Mathematical Practice support the idea that students should be actively engaged: solving problems, using tools, making arguments, and communicating their ideas. If the definition of proficiency has changed, shouldn't our vision of the math classroom change too? An effective math classroom may be noisier than we remember, with students collaborating to solve rich problems and share their thinking. Students may be exploring numbers with blocks or counters rather than simply with paper and pencil. The teacher may be moving through the classroom joining groups rather than being stationed by a board at the front of the room (see Figure I.2). We will look in more detail at this in Chapter 2.

Figure I.2 Teachers are actively engaged in discussing math ideas with students, probing for explanations and justifications.

How to Get There: This Book and the Math in Practice Series

The shifts we want to see in math teaching and learning require changes from everyone involved: you as the administrator, the teachers you work with, the students they teach, and the parents and community around those students. Math in Practice is designed to help you and your teams make these shifts.

ABOUT THE MATH IN PRACTICE SERIES

The Math in Practice series explores the teaching of mathematics across grades K–5. The eight-book series highlights what is taught in K–5 math, including both content standards and practice standards, and shares a wealth of teaching strategies and activities. But it is more than a compilation of activities and resources for teaching math; it is a guide for reflecting about math teaching. It provides a means for teachers to consider and process the changes in math teaching and determine how best to make those changes in their own teaching.

The *Guide for Teachers* is the central book of the Math in Practice series. It is designed to share instructional strategies and promote reflection about the teaching of elementary mathematics. It explores a wealth of research-informed instructional strategies that promote math learning, such as deep teacher questioning, multiple representations, math talk, formative assessment, differentiating instruction, making connections between math ideas, integrating problem solving into content lessons, and setting a real-world context for math skills. In order to promote reflection about these practices, the *Guide for Teachers* contains a set of reflective questions that can be used to prompt discussions at faculty study groups or simply for teachers to think about on their own. Discussing classroom observations, hearing the insights of colleagues, and collaboratively planning lessons help teachers begin to understand these strategies and make them their own.

The *Guide for Teachers* provides the foundation for the accompanying grade-level books, which allow teachers to visualize the teaching strategies with grade-specific content. Rather than simply being a compilation of lesson ideas, these books provide specific support to teachers including discussions of the math concepts for teachers who may not have a strong background with fractions or decimals or place value concepts but are now being asked to teach these concepts for understanding rather than memorization. In the Thinking Through a Lesson feature, included for each critical grade-level topic, the lesson designers share their thinking about how and why they chose to create the lesson in the way they did, helping teachers understand not only how to execute an activity or lesson, but how to think about, adapt, and design their own lessons based on a deeper understanding of math content and pedagogy. These books provide a wealth of lesson ideas and formative assessment tasks but are unique in that they also provide ongoing professional development as teachers reflect on the lessons and extend their thinking about teaching math.

ABOUT THIS BOOK

This book, *A Guide for Administrators*, offers a unique view of the teaching of elementary math from the perspectives of the district administrator, school-based administrator, and math coach. It explores your role as a leader in guiding change in our math classrooms and offers a wealth of ideas and resources to support you.

This book offers many ideas for moving your schools and districts toward this change. We examine such topics as

- the critical roles of the district math leader, school administrator, and math coach in moving the math program forward
- school and district program decisions that strengthen the math program
- what to look for in math classrooms during walk-throughs and classroom observations
- ways to support teachers as they make changes in their teaching practices
- how to involve teachers in analyzing school math data or student work and then determining next steps
- ideas for designing comprehensive math professional development programs and options for a variety of math professional learning experiences
- ways to effectively include parents in the math program.

Throughout the book, you will find ideas and resources to help you explore opportunities for positive change. Additional resources are available on the accompanying website: http://hein.pub/MathinPractice. You will notice thumbnails throughout the book that give you a quick glimpse of some of the accompanying materials. See page 133 for the full list of online resources.

To access the online resources, visit http://hein.pub/MathinPractice. Enter your email address and password (or click "Create a New Account" to set up an account). Once you have logged in, enter keycode MIPGA and click "Register".

We have known for a number of years that we have to change the way math is taught, yet that change is happening very slowly. How do we lead that change within our school or district? What can we do to enhance math learning and support our teachers to embrace and sustain meaningful change?

Through reflection about what we teach, who we teach, and how we teach, we are challenged to expand our notions about elementary school mathematics and embrace a new vision for math teaching. As our teachers expand their teaching practices, build positive dispositions about math, and examine critical math content and processes, they become more skilled and confident as teachers of mathematics. As we examine our program decisions about our elementary school math programs and open our minds to new ways to structure math classrooms, we move our schools closer to the vision of what a math classroom should be. The chapters ahead will guide our transition to that vision.

For additional reading about math teaching and learning, try the following:

National Research Council. 2001. *Adding It Up: Helping Children Learn Mathematics.* Washington, DC: National Academy Press.

National Council of Supervisors of Mathematics. 2014. *It's Time: Themes and Imperatives for Mathematics Education.* Bloomington, IN: Solution Tree Press.

National Governors Association Center for Best Practices and Council of Chief State School Officers. 2010. *Common Core State Standards for Mathematics.* Accessed on December 9, 2015. www.corestandards.org/assets/CCSSI_Math%20Standards.pdf.

National Council of Teachers of Mathematics. 1991. *Professional Standards for Teaching Mathematics,* Reston, VA: NCTM.

————. 2000. *Principles and Standards for School Mathematics.* Reston, VA: NCTM.

————. 2014. *Principles to Actions: Ensuring Mathematical Success for All.* Reston, VA: NCTM.

Leading a Math Program

Our goal is to build a strong elementary math program in which all of our students have opportunities to learn mathematics and feel positive about their experiences, but how do we get there? What program decisions strengthen math teaching and learning in our buildings? Who guides those decisions? Who ensures that mathematics has a strong emphasis within our schools?

Who Leads the Math Program?

The success of school and district math programs is a collaborative effort in which district administrators, principals, math coaches, teachers, parents, and staff all play a role. Involving varied stakeholders in math decisions helps ensure that the program is focused on the right priorities and continues to move forward.

THE ROLE OF DISTRICT LEADERS

District math leaders are mathematics specialists. They are aware of current math standards and are knowledgeable about math content and pedagogy. As school leaders strive to understand the changes in math standards and teaching strategies, the support of these specialists is invaluable. Their ability to offer specific

9

math insights helps school-based leaders make informed program decisions, support their teachers who struggle with math content or teaching, analyze math data to identify school needs, or identify related professional development needs and resources.

THE ROLE OF SCHOOL LEADERS

School-based administrators lead the learning programs within the school. They design the school schedule; determine which teachers teach math and at what grade levels; oversee the purchasing of math resources for the building; observe, evaluate, and support teachers; and manage the day-to-day business of teaching children mathematics. These are the instructional leaders of our schools. But their focus is on much more than mathematics, and they may or may not have a strong background in the subject. School-based content specialists, including coaches, lead teachers, and interventionists, work with both administrators and teachers to support strong math education programs.

The Power of an Instructional Coach

What team would be successful without a coach to guide it? Many districts employ elementary mathematics specialists, or math coaches, to provide teachers with the guidance and support they need to build their content knowledge, refine their instructional strategies, analyze their students' needs, and align their teaching with current standards.

The Association of Mathematics Teacher Educators (AMTE), the Association of State Supervisors of Mathematics (ASSM), the National Council of Supervisors of Mathematics (NCSM), and the National Council of Teachers of Mathematics (NCTM) issued a joint position statement recommending the use of such specialists, summarizing the role as "to enhance the teaching, learning, and assessing of mathematics to improve student achievement."[1] Most elementary building leaders acknowledge that reading specialists are indispensable. With the many mathematics-related changes facing our elementary teachers, and the acknowledgement that

---

[1] National Council of Teachers of Mathematics. *The Role of the Elementary Mathematics Specialists in the Teaching and Learning of Mathematics*, p. 1. http://www.nctm.org/Standards-and-Positions/ Position-Statements/The-Role-of-Elementary-Mathematics-Specialists-in-the-Teaching-and- Learning-of-Mathematics/.

many of them do not have strong backgrounds in the content of this subject, the same need must be true for mathematics specialists.

Math coaches should have extensive understanding of math content and math teaching and possess the leadership skills to transmit that knowledge to colleagues. Increasingly, this is a dedicated position within an individual school, in which the math coach supports all teachers as they build their content knowledge and refine their teaching skills, provides focused support to new or struggling teachers, monitors student progress, organizes schoolwide programs, manages math resources, and has an instrumental role in guiding the school's math program. Some districts modify this role (e.g., a highly skilled math classroom teacher with a reduced schedule that allows time to work with other teachers on a part-time basis or a position shared by schools with the coach rotating between schools, providing support as time allows). It is clear, however, that the less time a coach is available to teachers within a building, the less comprehensive her role can be and likely the less impact she may have on math teaching and learning. Particularly as we work to transform math teaching and rethink elementary math programs, having an individual who works with teachers to plan, co-teach, lead data discussions, develop interventions, communicate trends and best practices, answer questions, share ideas, or brainstorm solutions provides a necessary support to moving forward with change.

See the online resources for sample position descriptions.

Mathematics Leadership Committee

Most schools have school improvement teams, leadership teams, and various committees to guide school and district programs. The addition of a mathematics leadership committee helps chart a course for continuous mathematics program improvement. The committee provides an opportunity for members to gain leadership experience while also providing the following:

- Support for school improvement—The leadership group can work to review performance data and recommend areas of focus for the school improvement plan. The committee can support the development of specific strategies, data collection, and goal/target setting.
- Identification of professional development needs—The leadership committee can review achievement data and work to identify and plan for mathematics professional development. See Chapter 4 for more ideas about planning, organizing, and sustaining professional development.

- Review and recommend instructional resources—The math leadership committee can work to identify exemplary mathematics instructional resources. The group can also review resources and make recommendations for material purchases as well as suggestions for housing, inventorying, or sharing materials.

- Support for parent involvement—The committee can help build and maintain relationships with families through communicating what is changing in math instruction and why, and by organizing events such as family math nights. See Chapter 5 for more ideas about supporting parents and community.

- Support a positive school climate—The committee can play a pivotal role in supporting the mathematics environment and philosophy in the building. The group can identify opportunities for student and staff celebrations and schoolwide mathematics themes.

- Advocate for mathematics—The leadership committee advocates for mathematics. It places mathematics as a priority within the building and ensures that mathematics instruction's needs are discussed.

It is wise to have diverse perspectives and experiences on a leadership committee. Since every school is unique, we cannot name specific roles and individuals here, but some people and personalities to keep in mind include

- Math advocates—These are the teachers who live and breathe mathematics. They see math as much more than steps and procedures. Their classroom is mathematically engaging. They bring mathematics passion and energy to the group.

- Math worriers—These staff members may be afraid of mathematics or dislike it in general, or may be reluctant to change teaching methods that they feel have "always worked." They can shed light on misconceptions about the program and the needs of students and teachers who don't love math.

- Special educators and interventionists—These staff members advocate for students' diverse needs. They recognize that all students learn differently and reinforce that *all* students *can* learn math.

- Parents—Parents provide insight into the math experiences of their children. They offer ideas about communication with the community and offer their perspective on their children's needs.

- Students—Involving students themselves in the work of the committee may be appropriate for some topics and ensures that their perspectives are heard.
- Number crunchers—Number crunchers are staff members who love data and are able to figure out what it is telling us about math learning. They help remind us to look for evidence that supports our decisions.
- Motivators—Every building has unofficial leaders who rally the troops. Including these staff members in program decisions and engaging them in the process of building a strong math program ensures that their positive energy spills over to the rest of the staff.

You will want to balance grade-level or grade-band representation on the committee. It may make sense to include science, related arts, or technology staff as well. If a school has a large population of English language learners, including an ESL teacher would be helpful. A representative from the school district's mathematics staff may be helpful to ensure that the school's planning aligns with the district vision. And obviously, attending to racial, ethnic, and gender balance is critical.

Teachers

Teachers are, or can be, math leaders too. The teaching of mathematics demands a teacher who understands the math he is teaching; understands that mathematics instruction is balanced between concepts, procedures, and applications of mathematics; has confidence in his own abilities to teach math; and has a positive attitude about math.

Elementary teaching certification programs typically require teacher candidates to take only one or two mathematics courses. This preparation and certification does not always yield highly skilled mathematics teachers. It is nearly impossible to adequately train teachers in all of the skills needed to teach K–5 mathematics in just one or two college courses. Thus it's not surprising that many elementary teachers do not have the depth of understanding we might hope for. We can work to build all teachers' capacity through professional leaning opportunities (as described in Chapter 4), but in thinking through which teachers can serve as leaders among their peers, we look for teachers who

- are enthusiastic about mathematics, understanding that it is a rich and creative discipline
- eagerly and voluntarily take advantage of math-related professional-development opportunities

- deeply understand the mathematics content at their grade level and its connections to content at other levels
- understand the need to balance conceptual understanding, procedural knowledge, and application, and work to do this in their own teaching
- know how students tend to think about math, what misconceptions frequently arise, and how to help students rethink their ideas
- use formative assessment to guide teaching decisions
- believe that all students can learn math—and act in ways that demonstrate that belief
- establish and maintain positive relationships with colleagues.

Leading for Change

Having strong leaders who are committed to strong mathematics education is the first step. But what is it that those leaders need to do? Transforming our elementary math program is a multilayered undertaking that requires a deliberate plan and takes time. Do we need to rethink our philosophy about who can learn math? Do we need to revise our school schedule or develop new programs to match the importance we place on math within our schools? Do we need to review our curriculum, resources, and pacing schedules to determine if they match our current goals? Do we need to reflect on our teaching practices, replacing some outdated methods with ones that allow more students to make sense of mathematics? We may need to do all of these things.

As administrators, we need to be open to doing things differently than we have done in the past. We need to be willing to look carefully at our goals and redesign our school environment, schedules, resources, and programs to match those goals. We need to be willing to rethink our past beliefs, acknowledge that some of our traditional teaching methods may not get us to our goals, and let go of what is counterproductive. We need to guide teachers to examine and refine their teaching methods to be compatible with our new view of elementary mathematics. But understanding and embracing change is a struggle for many of us, administrators and teachers alike. How do we help ourselves, our teachers, and our school communities embrace change?

OBSTACLES TO CHANGE

Change is particularly difficult when any of the following are true:

- The purpose for the change is not clear.
- The amount of change feels overwhelming.
- There are strong habit patterns.
- There is a fear of failure.

Unclear Purpose

Without understanding why we need to change what we are doing, changing simply doesn't make sense. We may think, "The old ways were good enough for me. Why aren't they good enough for my students?" Some in your school community may see nothing wrong with traditional ways of teaching math like worksheets, drill and practice, and a focus only on correct answers, and if current school performance data is strong, it makes resistance to change even greater. Teachers may not yet have internalized the new expectations for students or thought deeply about how their teaching practices impact their students' success.

Before we can change, or ask others to change, we must be sure that the purpose for changing math teaching is clear to all. We can do this by providing opportunities for all staff to delve into the new standards, identifying the differences in math expectations for today's students, as well as providing opportunities for staff to discuss their own past experiences and beliefs about mathematics, considering whether they correspond with our goals for their students. Until teachers are able to buy in to why we are changing math standards and teaching practices, they are often unable to fully commit to those changes.

New standards are not the only reason for change. Review of student achievement data may indicate that our students are experiencing challenges with certain mathematics concepts. This review may also uncover achievement gaps between student groups or shed light on opportunities for more students to participate in accelerated mathematics. Whatever the specific reasons we identify for change, it is critical that everyone involved understand what those reasons are.

Feeling Overwhelmed

Large-scale change can feel overwhelming, and in recent years, we have asked teachers to embrace many new teaching practices. Should they focus on changing the assignments they give, the materials they use, the lessons they plan, or the way in which they interact with students? When asked to change too many things, confusion and frustration surface. The end result is that our teachers revert to practices they are comfortable with.

As leaders, we can help reduce this overwhelmed feeling by identifying some focus areas and allowing teachers time to digest, practice, and refine their teaching techniques. Focusing on major teaching strategies (e.g., teacher questioning, the use of models, formative assessment) can have dramatic effects across all math topics. Ongoing professional development, like faculty study groups, allows opportunities for teachers to discuss strategies as they work to implement them effectively, giving them the guidance and support needed to make the task feel more doable. Allowing room for making mistakes and reflecting on adjustments to teaching strategies support teachers to hang in when trying something new can be frustrating.

Note: These teaching strategies are addressed in depth in Math in Practice: A Guide for Teachers *and are highlighted in the grade-level books.*

Strong Habits

Many of us sat in math classrooms that were taught in the same way year after year. Unfortunately, it is difficult to break out of that pattern. It is so easy to simply revert back to comfortable patterns and teach math the way we were taught. This may be particularly true for teachers who are not fully comfortable with math themselves. We are much more likely to cling to familiar patterns when faced with something we find intimidating.

We can help our schools and teachers change their habits by having teachers set specific goals for what they would like to add, change, and delete from their teaching repertoire and then giving them ongoing opportunities to share their efforts, knowing that this change takes time. Having teachers attach sticky notes to their desks or teacher's guides with brief cues can be the constant reminder needed during the initial stages of making the change. For example, a teacher might put a note saying "turn and share" on her desk to remind herself to get all students answering questions rather than just calling on one student in the traditional "raise your hand" model. Providing ongoing checkpoints for teachers to discuss how they are doing, and to celebrate when the new practice feels natural, makes the change process a team effort.

Fear of Failure

Many elementary teachers lack confidence in their own math abilities. They may have mastered math computations by memorizing procedures but may feel inadequate and unsure of themselves when delving into deep discussions about math concepts, modeling math ideas, or applying math skills to solve problems. They are afraid they can't do it, and that fear can stop them from trying or cause them to abandon their efforts prematurely. And with today's focus on teacher evaluations, teachers may fear that if they try something and it doesn't work they'll be evaluated poorly. Sticking with the approaches they know feels safe.

Many adults have developed the mindset that they are not good at math or that math is an innate skill that they do not possess. If a teacher has this fixed mindset, he does not expect to succeed—and he does not expect all of his students to succeed and has an excuse for why some can't. Students with fixed mindsets have no reason to try, because they believe the goal of math success is unattainable for them. We are challenged to change this mindset, first within ourselves and then within our students.

Researcher Carol Dweck explains that the opposite of this fixed mindset is a growth mindset, based on the idea that we can improve our abilities through work and effort (Dweck 2007). In other words, success in math is not about being a "math person"; it is about experience and effort, not about being born with "math genes." It is up to us as leaders to make a growth mindset the foundational philosophy of our program. As our teachers embrace a growth mindset they are able to convey their beliefs to students. Knowing you can succeed, whether you are a teacher or student of mathematics, gives you hope of success.

We help foster a growth mindset in our teachers and a willingness to take risks by reducing their fear of being penalized for trying strategies that don't work immediately, providing opportunities for them to further develop their math knowledge through professional development experiences, and validating the connection between their effort and success.

The Big Decisions

An effective mathematics program is founded on decisions that are informed by data, research, classroom observations, and our past experiences as well as the experience of our staff. We will discuss more about how leaders can support change at the classroom level in future chapters, but let's now look at some of the larger-scale changes and decisions that school and district leaders need to consider to support effective mathematics instruction: decisions around school schedule, school structure, meeting the needs of our varied students (including intervention programs), and how we support and evaluate teachers. There are many ways to realize an effective mathematics program, and schools find success with different approaches, but the following discussions and suggestions can help inform these decisions.

SCHOOL SCHEDULE

Ask any math teacher what her number-one challenge is and the response is frequently a lack of time. What might our students achieve with an additional fifteen days of instruction? How about an extra thirty days or even as much as forty-five days? We may actually have that much time available in our daily schedule. A simple adjustment may come from the amount of time we allocate for mathematics. Over the course of 180 school days, adding five minutes to each math class equates to an additional fifteen days of math instruction! An extra fifteen minutes a day would equal forty-five extra days—a full nine-week quarter. How would finding additional time impact your students' success? It may seem impossible at first glance to fit anything more into a crowded school day, but finding five or ten minutes more might be a matter of rethinking transition times, streamlining school announcements or closing procedures, integrating content with language arts classes, shifting time from other content classes to mathematics, limiting or removing homeroom opening activities, or reworking lunch and recess schedules.

Timing

When we teach math during the day can also be important. It would be ideal to teach math early in the day, when students are freshest (see Figure 1.1). We all know the "after-lunch drain," and by the end of the day students and teachers both are often tired and lose focus. It is also important to allow for uninterrupted time for math instruction. While it is a good idea to weave math into other moments of the day (such as math discussions during morning meeting and quick math prompts at transition times), it is less helpful to have the math block interrupted by lunch or recess or disrupted by students being pulled out for music or other activities. Assemblies and special events should not always occur during math time.

See the online resources for sample school schedules.

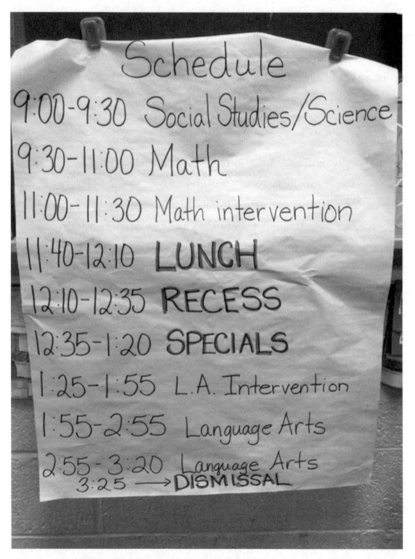

Figure 1.1 It is refreshing to see school schedules in which math and reading/language arts are shared priorities, with time devoted to instruction and interventions for each content area.

Other Scheduling Issues

Other factors related to designing a school schedule that impact math teaching and learning include the following:

- Collaborative planning—In recent years we have made great strides to provide teachers with collaborative planning time, recognizing the importance of teachers working together to plan effective instructions. Finding time to include these planning sessions as we design our school schedule has tremendous benefits. Collaborative planning can include teammates and co-teachers. School-based leaders can join collaborative planning sessions to stay informed about each grade level's progress and to monitor instructional successes and challenges. For considerations when designing collaborative planning meetings, ensuring they focus on standards and math learning, see Chapter 4.

- Co-teaching opportunities—Traditionally, students received additional academic support through classroom pull-out programs, but in recent years, the co-teaching model with a special educator working alongside the classroom teacher has gained momentum. While a co-teaching model reduces the student-teacher ratio and helps with classroom management, it can also have considerable impact on student achievement in mathematics. Arranging a schedule that allows for co-teaching should be a consideration as the school schedule is designed.

Above all, it is important to be willing to change when something is not working. It is wise to work with a leadership team on a yearly basis to review data on students' learning, as well as input from staff, to adjust schedules as needed to meet the needs of students and teachers. Making sure everyone knows and remembers that the instructional schedule is designed to maximize student learning helps all school staff remember that it is what is best for students that really matters.

SCHOOL STRUCTURE: CONSIDERING DEPARTMENTALIZATION

Departmentalization, also known as platooning, is nothing new. Middle school and high school teachers have been doing it as long as anyone can remember. But many of our elementary teachers are faced with the challenge of being a "jack of all trades." They are asked to be experts at teaching reading, writing, science, social studies, health, and mathematics. Is this always the wisest decision? Circumstances vary from school to school, but it is worth giving consideration to the idea of departmentalization at the elementary level.

Perhaps one of the greatest advantages to departmentalization is that it allows us to assign our highly skilled math teachers to grade levels rather than having every teacher at a level teach math regardless of his skills, experiences, or attitudes. Understanding the content at a deeper level enables specialized teachers to carefully scaffold learning, make connections to previous learning, and better differentiate for the needs of students who may need a review of past content or the challenge of more complex skills.

Lower cost and easier storage of math resources can also be an advantage. Schools may need to purchase fewer materials, such as manipulatives, because fewer students would be using them at any one time. Classrooms can be set up as math labs with materials and supplies organized and ready for student use. And teachers who have more experience with math content are more willing and better able to use the materials effectively to explore and model math ideas.

Schools have found success with different kinds of departmentalization. Some departmentalize only for grades 3 through 5, while in others, even first and second graders experience some form of departmentalization. Some have departmentalized for all content areas. Others have developed a modified form of departmentalization in which one teacher might handle reading, writing, and social studies for a group of students, while another teacher handles math and science for those same students. Students might spend the morning with one teacher and the afternoon with the other. This arrangement allows the two teachers to work together to support cross-content learning while still specializing in their own content areas.

The potential loss of connections is a common argument against departmentalization and one worth considering. Teachers often fear that departmentalization may create silos of learning in which ideas are isolated and disconnected, rather than offering the teacher opportunities to make connections between subjects throughout the day, what we refer to as "teachable moments." It is worth considering, though, that more skilled math teachers may be better able to make more meaningful connections and applications of mathematics. Well-designed collaborative-planning teams can also help ensure that teachers of different subjects work together to make these connections.

There is also concern that we lose the strength of our relationships. That is, our students lose the strong bond with their teacher because they spend less time with him or her in a departmentalized model. This is a reasonable concern, because the teacher-student relationship can be a very potent one, lasting a lifetime for some students. While the forging of a strong teacher-student bond can be important to a student's success, when done in a caring atmosphere, departmentalization may give students a chance to get support from a wider network of adults.

It will be up to you and your mathematics leadership team to assess the advantages and disadvantages of departmentalization for your own situations. Whatever decision is made, it should focus on giving students the best math experience possible at each grade level.

MEETING THE NEEDS OF VARIED STUDENTS

See more on this topic on the Math Forum Internet Library: http://mathforum .org/library/ed _topics/tracking/.

Students at any grade level have varied needs and abilities. When determining class rosters, it can be tempting to place like-ability students together. The assumption is that it is easier for a teacher to have a more cohesive ability group, but research does not support this approach. The method of tracking students, or placing them in ability-grouped classrooms, has not shown to be effective in promoting increased student achievement; in fact, students in low groups have been shown to stay in low groups. These groups also, unfortunately, often reflect and solidify racial and class differences within a school, which goes against all our goals for equity in instruction. With proper support for teachers, heterogeneous classrooms allow all students a better chance to succeed.

Planning for Intervention

See Math in Practice: A Guide for Teachers, Chapter 5, for ideas on flexible grouping and differentiation.

Rather than teaching all students the same lesson at the same pace, we have seen the need for flexible grouping in which classroom teachers provide small-group support as needed to enrich students who are ready to extend their learning and remediate for those who need additional support. It is vital to provide our teachers with the time and classroom support needed to allow them to work with small groups in the larger classroom setting (see Figure 1.2).

Figure 1.2 Small-group experiences within the math classroom allow teachers to provide additional support or enrichment as needed.

But sometimes, even the strongest classroom instruction is not enough to meet a student's needs. The U.S. Department of Education (2009) released the following series of recommendations for schools implementing intervention programs:

- Screen all students for potential math difficulties, and plan for interventions for those that need them. It is also important to monitor the progress of students who are receiving interventions and of other students who may be at risk.
- Interventions in grades K–5 should focus on a deep understanding of whole-number concepts (along with fractions and decimals in grades 4–5). Intervention sessions should include about ten minutes devoted to building fluency with basic computation facts as well.
- The additional instruction should be "explicit and systematic. This includes providing models of proficient problem solving, verbalization of thought

processes, guided practice, corrective feedback, and frequent cumulative review."[2]

- Instruction should include support for solving word problems based on underlying structures and many opportunities for students to work with different visual representations. Obviously, those working with students should understand and know how to use those representations as well.

- Instruction should be motivating, acknowledging that many students in tier 2 and tier 3 interventions have experienced discouragement and failure and need activities that are engaging and celebrate their successes.

When planning for intervention, it is important to remember that intervention time is *additional* time with mathematics for students who need it. It should not be a replacement that deprives students of their regular instructional time. Many schools have designed schedules that allow students to have a second helping of math during the school day. In some schools, before- or after-school programs have been organized to provide additional math experience for targeted students, while other schools have found Saturday schools or summer learning opportunities helpful. It is our responsibility to think creatively and find ways to provide additional math opportunities to students who struggle with understanding critical skills and concepts.

While paraprofessionals and volunteers can help, highly skilled teachers are obviously the first choice for leading intervention groups. They possess the content understanding and teaching skills to identify where learning gaps or confusions may occur and remediate as needed. Special education teachers can also be valuable in providing support for students with specific identified needs.

Advanced Students

Targeted small-group mathematics time is valuable for students who are ready for additional challenge. As with students who may be struggling, these students benefit from teaching by an experienced, skilled math teacher, though properly trained paraprofessionals and outside volunteers can also support them. Rather

---

[2] U.S. Department of Education. 2009. *Assisting Students Struggling with Mathematics: Response to Intervention (RtI) for Elementary and Middle Schools*, p. 6.

than bumping these students to the next grade level's content, as was once the standard approach, there are many opportunities to enrich their learning through problems, explorations, and investigations that challenge their thinking and add depth to their learning.

English Language Learners

English language learners benefit from our attention to specific teaching practices that help them understand and make sense of math ideas. Using visual images to support the language being used, focusing on critical math vocabulary, using manipulatives to explore ideas and prompt discussions about math concepts, and connecting abstract ideas to real-world contexts are all beneficial strategies. Respecting each student's native language and being cognizant of the need to move beyond language-only strategies for presenting math ideas helps us better meet their needs.

See Math in Practice: A Guide for Teachers, Chapter 5, for ideas on flexible grouping and differentiation.

TEACHER EVALUATION

Teacher evaluation is a stressful process for many teachers, particularly if their teaching appointment may be affected by the results. Teachers trust that administrators know what to look for in math classrooms, that they are able to identify which strategies and interactions indicate strong teaching and promote student learning.

As school and district leaders, we count on our ability to identify successes and pinpoint concerns during teacher observations. These observations then guide our efforts to offer suggestions and support teachers as they improve and refine math teaching. In the next chapter, we discuss ways to gather information about math teaching and highlight what to look for in elementary math classrooms.

For additional information on the role of elementary mathematics specialists:

The Role of Elementary Mathematics Specialists in the Teaching and Learning of Mathematics position statement at www.nctm.org/Standards-and-Positions/Position-Statements/The-Role-of-Elementary-Mathematics-Specialists-in-the-Teaching-and-Learning-of-Mathematics/.

The Elementary Math Specialists and Teacher Leaders Project at www.mathspecialists.org.

Questions for Reflection

- Who are the mathematics leaders in our building?

- Who is on our mathematics leadership committee? What work will they lead?

- How does our school schedule impact mathematics instruction time and ultimately our student achievement?

- When do we teach mathematics? When do we schedule assemblies? Do we have mathematics on half days?

- Should our best mathematics teachers teach math to all students?

- What topics do we focus on during intervention? Is counting coins as important as adding two-digit numbers in second grade?

- How is intervention different from initial instruction?

- Who provides our mathematics interventions? How well do they understand mathematics content and pedagogy?

- Do we meet the needs of successful students? Do we challenge them appropriately?

Gathering Insights About Math Teaching Through Observation

To ensure that math standards are being addressed, that both content and process skills are being developed, and that students are learning math in thoughtful, interactive, and positive ways, we need a clear picture of how math is being taught within our classrooms. Through formal observations and coaching sessions as well as informal visits and walk-throughs, we as leaders can gather important data that will help us identify school and teacher needs, plan professional development, and support teachers as they work to improve their teaching. This chapter will address two key questions: How do you recognize an effective math lesson when you see it, and, more importantly, how do you guide a teacher who may not be teaching at a level that meets your expectations?

How Do We Know a Good Math Lesson When We See It?

What do we hope to see and hear when we step into a math classroom? As our focus has shifted from memorizing to understanding and from calculating to applying, we have recognized instructional strategies that are better suited to these goals.

SHIFTS IN WHAT WE EXPECT

Today, we know the following are less effective ways to teach math:

- extensive periods of quiet practice
- frequent use of tedious worksheets
- seating arrangements that inhibit cooperative learning and discussion
- extensive teacher lectures with a focus on telling the steps for math procedures
- rigid approaches to computation or problem solving
- teaching one way for all students
- assessment by tests and quizzes administered only after teaching is completed
- neutral or subversive comments about mathematics.

Those practices are not conducive to building mathematical thinkers and problem solvers or to the development of students' number sense and their understanding of math skills and concepts.

Figure 2.1 A look into today's math classrooms reveals students actively engaged in making sense of mathematics.

Instead, we would rather see and hear

- lots of math talk by students
- students involved in hands-on and visual explorations of math concepts that go beyond teacher demonstration
- students working together to discuss their thinking and solve math problems
- balanced instruction that focuses on skills and processes
- opportunities for students to discuss varied approaches
- frequent discussions about what students notice, developing rules and making connections between math ideas
- varied teaching formats and additional support for students who need it
- ongoing and varied assessment throughout the teaching process
- positive and engaging comments about mathematics, even when it requires perseverance.

"LOOK FORS" IN THE ELEMENTARY MATH CLASSROOM

As we observe math classrooms, we look for evidence that teaching is more than delivering a textbook lesson. We look at the interactions between teacher and students, the on-the-spot decisions made by the teacher to keep learning progressing, and the ways in which the teacher brings math ideas to light through talk, visuals, and connections to past learning. More specifically, here are some key features we would hope to see in an effective math classroom.

See Math in Practice: A Guide for Teachers for a more in-depth look at effective math teaching strategies.

Look for a Clear Focus on Math Standard(s)

Without a clear focus on the standard being addressed, teaching can get side-tracked. Teachers and students should be aware of the standard, or standards, that drive the lesson, as well as the connection to standards addressed in previous grades.

- What standard(s) is being addressed?
- Is the standard appropriate for the grade level and is it conveyed in student-friendly terms?
- Do the activities and teaching strategies focus on the standard?
- Is there evidence of both process and content standards being addressed?
- What connections are being made to standards addressed in previous grades?

Look for Students Actively Engaged in Learning

Engagement is likely the most critical component of teaching and learning. Students learn when they are engaged in the lesson.

- Are the math tasks high-quality and worthwhile?
- Are teachers guiding the explorations, allowing students to think for themselves?
- Are all students answering questions (e.g., are turn-and-share strategies being used rather than one student answering the question)?
- Are students allowed time for productive struggle? Are they praised for effort and perseverance?

Look for Deep and Focused Teacher Questioning

Through deep questions teachers are able to probe, scaffold, and extend students' thinking.

- What is the depth of teacher questioning? Are teachers going beyond asking for answers to asking for explanations and justifications? Does the teacher ask probing questions (e.g., Why? How? What if . . .? What does that mean? Will that always work?) to stimulate students' thinking?
- Does the teacher ask questions that focus students' thinking on a specific understanding or insight?
- Is time given for students to formulate their ideas (e.g., wait time or partner discussions)?

Look for Communication About Math Ideas

It is through talk that students develop mathematical reasoning and problem-solving skills, process their own ideas, hear the ideas of others, and extend and refine their own mathematical thinking.

- What does the teacher talk sound like? Is the teacher using think-alouds, revoicing students' ideas, clarifying concepts with examples, and making connections?
- What does the student talk sound like? Do students have frequent opportunities to explain and justify their thinking? Are student-to-student conversations encouraged?

- Are students encouraged to discuss and share observations and insights about math investigations?
- Are students pushed to elaborate on their thinking and to comment on others' ideas?
- Is precision expected when students talk about math? Are students being asked to use appropriate math terms and precisely explain their thinking?
- Is flawed reasoning investigated and discussed?

Look for Posing and Solving Problems as an Integral Part of Math Instruction

Problem solving should not be seen as an afterthought, something we do at the end of a lesson. Problems should be integrated into all parts of lessons. Connections to real situations through problem contexts helps students make sense of math skills and understand when and how to apply the skills.

- Are connections made between math skills and real situations?
- Are problems integrated into skills teaching to set a context for math skills and concepts?
- Do students discuss strategies for comprehending and making sense of problems?
- Is modeling problems with manipulatives or drawings encouraged?
- Do students have the opportunity to share, discuss, and explain their varied strategies and justify their solutions?

Look for a Focus on Building Understanding

Understanding math concepts and procedures is foundational. Through investigations, representations, and math talk we help students build a solid foundation. For example, rather than teaching computation skills as a step-by-step process to memorize, we first explore the skills using visual models and strategies based on our understanding of place value, operations, and properties. Then, the steps of the procedure make sense.

- Are lessons focused on developing understanding, not just memorizing?
- Are flexible strategies encouraged, and do discussions occur to connect those strategies to a basic understanding of numbers and operations?

- Are students encouraged to use tools (e.g., hands-on materials, paper and pencil, hundred charts, number lines . . .) as they explore math ideas?
- Are models and math talk used to promote understanding?

Look for Varied Representations of Math Thinking

Students learn about math by creating models of math concepts and processes. They benefit from opportunities to visualize math ideas through manipulatives, drawings, and acting out situations as well as using abstract numbers and symbols. These varied representations help them develop insights about the big ideas being explored.

- Does the teacher include visual models when discussing math ideas and demonstrating math skills and concepts?
- Are students expected to model math ideas and share and explain their models?
- Are manipulatives readily available for student use?
- Does the teacher facilitate discussions that compare and contrast varied representations?
- Are connections made between symbolic representations and visual models?

Look for Assessment as an Integral Part of Instruction

Through ongoing assessment, information is gathered about what students know and are able to do, allowing teachers to modify math instruction to meet their needs. Is formative assessment evident?

- Is the teacher gathering evidence of student understanding during instruction? Are opportunities built into the lesson that allow the teacher to check for understanding?
- Is the teacher making on-the-spot decisions based on what students are saying or doing? Is the teacher posing questions to probe or extend thinking, revisiting skills, or clarifying ideas, or pulling small groups of students to reteach or enrich?

Look for Attention to the Needs of Diverse Students

Not all learners in our classrooms have the same prior knowledge or learn math in the same way or at the same pace. Is there attention to the needs of all learners?

- Is the teacher attending to different skill levels within the classroom? Are modifications in the task or teaching evident (e.g., to remediate or enrich learning)?
- Do some students need, and receive, additional support through small groups or adjusted pacing?
- Are tools available to support the success of some students?

See the online resources for highlights of these questions that can be used as a reminder when conducting observations, classroom visits, and discussions.

How Can We Support Teachers to Meet These Expectations?

The more we know about the way math is taught within our classrooms, the more likely we will be to offer productive suggestions that enhance and refine that teaching. Once we have a vision of what a math classroom should look like and sound like, the next step is to get into those classrooms to see if reality matches that vision. Both informal walk-throughs and more formal observations and coaching sessions give us key information about math teaching in our schools and enable us to support teachers more effectively.

THE POWER OF INFORMAL CLASSROOM WALK-THROUGHS

Brief classroom visits or walk-throughs allow us to gain a picture of instruction over time and throughout the school or district. The observations we gather provide a starting point for discussions with individual teachers or with the staff as a whole. They give us insight into what might become school or district initiatives. Frequent walk-throughs help teachers feel comfortable with our regular presence in their classrooms. Rather than teaching being done behind closed doors, the teaching process becomes transparent, and more formal observations will produce less pressure when teachers know their school leaders see their day-to-day teaching, instead of having everything ride on one particular day's lesson.

We might conduct focused walk-throughs at a particular grade level in order to gather data about a specific initiative or concern (e.g., observing intermediate students as they work to make sense of operations with fractions or visiting primary classrooms to gather insights about how students are doing with math talk). General walk-throughs, however, simply to observe the teaching and learning in all classrooms, should be a routine part of each week (see Figure 2.2).

Figure 2.2 When principals frequently visit classrooms throughout the school, students become accustomed to having them join the math discussions.

Plan to spend only a brief period of time in the room, maybe ten or fifteen minutes. You will not see a complete lesson in this time, of course. If you are visiting during the initial part of the lesson, you may see only how the teacher introduces a topic or transitions into the lesson from the previous day's skills. If you visit the room during the middle part of the lesson, you may only see students engaged in collaborative problem solving. But over time, you have the opportunity to see the teaching at all points in the lesson, and these snapshots of teaching and learning form a clear picture of what routinely happens in that classroom. Because these walk-throughs are usually not scheduled, they provide a look at authentic teaching.

What to Focus On

During a walk-through we look and listen for teaching strategies, content objectives, student engagement, and evidence of student learning.

- Observe and listen to students—This might include gazing at what they are working on, listening to their conversations with peers, or even asking them to explain what they are learning, if it is not disruptive to the lesson (see Figure 2.3).
  - ◉ What are they doing? What are they saying?
  - ◉ Are they engaged?
  - ◉ Do they understand the math?
- Consider the math being taught.
  - ◉ What is the objective?
  - ◉ Is it a critical math topic? Is the lesson standards-based?
  - ◉ Does the lesson address both math content and process?

Figure 2.3 Classroom walk-throughs include observing math tasks and listening to students' conversations.

- Observe the teaching strategies and teacher-student interactions.
  - What instructional strategies are being used?
  - What types of questions are being asked?
  - Is the teacher providing visual or hands-on opportunities?
  - Is there evidence of differentiation?
  - Is the teacher making connections between ideas?
  - What decisions is the teacher making? Are they appropriate decisions?
- Look at the classroom environment.
  - Are math materials evident? Are centers available?
  - Is the classroom designed for student interaction?
  - What items in the room provide evidence of past activities or instructional strategies?

Following up on Classroom Walk-Throughs

These brief visits do not require formal feedback to teachers, but brief verbal comments, if not disruptive, or brief written comments offer you an opportunity to praise teaching strategies or ask questions to prompt teacher reflection. For instance, if students got stuck, what did the teacher do and what questions did she ask that motivated students to persevere? When students are unable to move forward in a problem-solving situation, the questions asked by the teacher may make all the difference in moving them to a successful solution. It is extremely motivating for teachers when you share that you noticed those questions and their moves. Some administrators simply leave a sticky note on the teacher's desk with a brief comment about the task, the teaching, or the student interactions. Acknowledging and celebrating the good things teachers do on a daily basis promotes a positive environment and opens the door to constructive feedback.

While many administrators hesitate to take notes during walk-throughs—it can make the visit feel more evaluative—it can be helpful to jot down notes following the visits while our observations are fresh in our mind. In particular, it can be useful to make note of trends that either show improvement and attention to school initiatives or highlight concerns and possible focal points for future school reflection. In this way, we are able to reflect on what we have seen and consider ways to use the observations to support individual teachers or to promote faculty reflection. Often math coaches join school administrators for walk-throughs or conduct their own walk-throughs, so they are well aware of math teaching throughout the building and can discuss their insights with the administrator and collaborate on next steps. Questions you might think about after doing walk-throughs with your teachers include the following:

- Which teachers need additional support in refining their teaching practices?
- Which teachers might be asked to share effective strategies with colleagues?
- What resources might be helpful in the classrooms?
- What skills and concepts are students struggling to understand?
- What schoolwide concerns might be put on an agenda for faculty discussions?

Conducting walk-throughs with math coaches or district leaders is an opportunity to calibrate our understanding of current mathematics practices. It also provides an opportunity to align with district expectations. Conducting walk-throughs with teachers creates a similar benefit. In doing so, teachers have insight into what you look for as you visit. They also have an opportunity to reflect on their own practice.

FORMAL OBSERVATION AND CONFERENCING

Formal observations are a common part of life in our schools. Frequently these are used as part of teacher evaluation, and your school or district may require a specific procedure or set of criteria. However, formal observations also play a critical role in improving instruction.

This kind of observation is most successful when it involves a preobservation discussion and a postobservation conference in which you and the teacher meet to discuss the lesson and plan how the teacher can shift or further develop her instruction in the future. These observations might be conducted by a school or district administrator or by a math coach.

Before You Observe

A preobservation conference allows the teacher to briefly share his goals and summarize his lesson and the context of that lesson. Asking what math standards have been addressed prior to the lesson and which will be addressed after places the lesson within a content progression and helps us interpret both teacher decisions and student actions more accurately.

For coaching conferences, the preconference is the time to discuss specifics that you will be observing. What are you observing for, or what does the teacher want you to look for? Decide together what you will be focusing on (e.g., pacing of the lesson, students' understanding of the math concept, types of questions asked, student engagement in the lesson, use and management of manipulatives, and so on). This decision will help you plan for what information you will collect during the observation. If lesson pacing is the issue, for instance, you might plan to jot down the time frequently throughout the lesson. If teacher questioning is the focus, you might decide to record each question asked. Knowing the specific emphasis of the observation allows you to focus your attention on those aspects of instruction and gather more pertinent observations.

There are other considerations you might discuss during the preobservation conference, like the following:

- What strengths do your students have in mathematics? What needs do they have?
- How does the lesson fit with our curriculum?
- What misconceptions do you think students will have? How might you address them?
- How will you and your students represent the mathematics?
- What questions are you planning to ask?
- How will you structure the class? Will you use small groups or cooperative learning?
- How will you assess what students have learned?
- How will you close the lesson?

During the Observation

The observation is about gathering objective data about the math teaching and learning taking place in the classroom. The goal is not to ensure that the teacher precisely follows her lesson plan but to observe the teacher's moves and responses to students' learning. It is the way in which teachers adjust, revoice, differentiate, and modify their plans on the spot that alerts us to their ability to teach math for understanding. (It is important to make this clear to the teacher as well; this clarification helps reduce anxiety and encourages the teacher to make in-the-moment decisions more confidently.)

It can be tough to write as we watch and listen to both teacher and students, but our notes are critical as we later analyze the lesson.

- Record the math standard that is the focus of the lesson.
- Briefly record main teaching points, including any significant teacher or student quotes.
- Record times periodically throughout the lesson in case you need to analyze the lesson pacing, determine how much time students spend at centers, or reflect on another time-related issue.
- Develop symbols to note positive comments or actions (+) or negative comments or actions (–) or comments or actions that you may want to ask questions about (?) because they were confusing or unnecessary.
- If you are focusing on the types of questions asked, record each question, or note when teachers ask questions that call for answer only (A) or answers and explanation/elaboration (E).
- If observing for teacher-to-student or student-to-student interactions, make a note of each time T-S or S-S talk happens.
- If you are observing for the teaching of problem solving, record when teachers prompt students to restate, model, or explain their strategies.

Some additional tips for successful observations include:

- Asking the teacher to provide you with a copy of all handouts helps you follow the lesson from the students' perspective.
- While some observers tend to sit quietly in a corner of the room, it might be helpful at times to walk through the room to look at what students are doing.
- Remember to focus on evidence and avoid making inferences.
- Take pictures to support your write-up.
- Consider taking brief videos with a phone or tablet and sharing them with the teacher prior to your postobservation conference. Ask teachers to reflect on what they notice about their own teaching. Consider asking them to look for evidence of aspects that you were looking for, including questioning or student engagement. Any part of the lesson can be recorded. This is simply a window into the lesson. It doesn't need to be comprehensive.

Preparing for the Postobservation Conference

Before the postobservation conference, review the data you have gathered, prioritize your concerns, and decide which ones to address during the conference. A laundry list of concerns may be overwhelming and unproductive; just as students shut down when they are faced with an overload of information, many teachers shut down when they are overwhelmed by the number of issues to rework within the lesson.

It is important to plan for a postconference that can open a respectful, productive dialogue about the lesson. As a starting point, identify what happened that

- enhanced student learning—plan to praise what the teacher did in these moments
- hindered or distracted from student learning—these can be points to discuss, and the basis for plans for improvement
- had no major impact on student learning one way or the other—these might be unnecessary parts of the lesson.

If you are an administrator who is not a math specialist, you may not feel qualified to offer specific teaching suggestions. Involving a school or district math coach or specialist in reviewing observation notes and planning the postconference can be helpful; they can provide suggestions as well as help you identify potential areas of strength or need for teachers. Pursuing an opportunity to do an observation with your district mathematics leader to calibrate the process may be a helpful option as well.

And asking the teacher to reflect on the lesson following the observation helps him prepare for the conversation you will have during the postobservation conference.

Conducting the Postobservation Conference

During the conference, our goal is to effectively convey our commendations and our concerns and begin a dialogue about the lesson. We want the teacher to recognize what needs to change and be willing to discuss it with us.

Beginning the conference by asking the teacher's perspective on how the lesson went ("What went well? What might you change?") allows her to share her thoughts about the lesson and articulate what may not have gone as planned, suggesting adjustments to the lesson. This approach shows respect for the teacher's knowledge of math content and pedagogy. Knowing our teachers, like knowing our students, is critical for this stage of the observation process. We must be mindful of those who perceive that what they do is always the best or those that are much harder on themselves. In some cases, it may be better to forego any questions that are perceived as evaluative (e.g., What went well?) and simply focus on questions like "If you were to teach the lesson again, what would you do differently?" This open question jump-starts a discussion about the lesson without any evaluative implications.

It is always best to begin conferences with the positive. Design some specific positive statements that emphasize cause and effect: *"When you presented the math problem about the school fair, the students were excited by the familiar context. They couldn't wait to get started on it."* This helps teachers see that the student excitement didn't just happen on its own; it was caused by their decision to personalize the problem to a familiar situation. Rather than being a blanket praise statement ("Good problem!), this praise specified what was good about the problem and why.

Designing feedback statements about your concerns is often more difficult. When presenting a concern, we consider how that message might be best received. Providing teachers with objective statements of what we observed and then asking them to figure out why certain student behaviors occurred challenges them to determine connections between what they did and what the students did (cause/effect) and can be a powerful way to spur insights. Ask questions about any confusing activities or actions (e.g., "Why did you . . .?" or "Help me understand why . . ."). Many times, lessons do not go as planned, but if a teacher recognizes the problem and has insight into what she could do to address it, there may be no need for us to share those same concerns and recommendations. We certainly offer suggestions when a teacher has difficulty figuring out what she might have been done differently, but first asking her to consider modifications to her teaching puts the responsibility on her to find ways to enhance her practice.

Questions such as the following can help you probe teachers' thinking when lessons don't go as well as they, or we, would like:

Why did you . . .?

What did you expect your students to be able to do?

Were you surprised when . . .?

Allow teachers to explain their actions and decisions to help you make sense of what you saw. Share your objective observations, and ask teachers what they might have done to get a different response from students. Be sure that any concerns can be substantiated with observable data and are followed with suggestions for improvement (e.g., rather than saying the students "weren't engaged," refer to the four students who were building towers with the manipulatives, the five students who didn't know which center to go to, or the small group that was talking about what happened at recess). Brainstorm together (and perhaps with a math coach or specialist) ways to address the concern in future lessons.

Consider the following examples:

> **Example 1:** Ms. Alexander gave the class fifteen minutes to complete exercises 1–10 on page 52 of their workbooks. Several students did all ten computations but made the same procedural error in each one. Three students were done in ten minutes and drew pictures on their papers for the remaining five minutes.

The key is to have the teacher consider her actions (the assignment she gave) and the resulting student behaviors. What did she notice? Why did she think it happened?

Some specific questions you might consider in this example:

- How might she have identified the error some students were making, and what could she have done to address it? Perhaps she could have had students do two problems to start and circulated as they worked so that she could identify a small group that needed further instruction while other students completed the remaining problems.
- What was her plan for when students finish work early? Did she have a center or other math task for students to work on? If so, why did students not make use of it? If not, this might be something she could add to her plans for future lessons.

> **Example 2:** Ms. Alexander asked students to justify their answers but told all students to think for one minute prior to answering. Then, she asked students to share their thinking with a partner. All students were engaged in talking about their ideas with a partner. Several students shared thoughtful justifications with the class.

In this case, asking the teacher why she thought the students were able to share such thoughtful justifications can help her identify areas of strength she can build on in the future and techniques that she can use more frequently in other lessons.

Planning for Follow-Up

As you conclude the conference, collaborate with the teacher to develop an action plan—a few goals to work on in the coming weeks. Record the goals discussed and the plan to address them. Consider additional ways in which you might support this teacher.

- Should the teacher co-plan with a grade-level team member?
- Would it be helpful for the teacher to observe a colleague's teaching?
- Would the teacher benefit from additional support with math content?
- Does this teacher need to develop skills with a specific instructional strategy?
- Would this teacher benefit from additional math manipulatives or classroom resources?
- How might the teacher work with the school math coach or district math specialist?
    - Could the math coach co-plan and co-teach some lessons with this teacher?
    - Would it be helpful to have the math coach do some coaching observations in this classroom?
- Should you offer to observe at another time to assess progress?
- Should you set up a meeting to revisit the action plan?

End the conference on a positive note with a plan for future assistance.

Through the observation and conference process, teachers gain opportunities to reflect on their teaching and improve their self-evaluation skills. The goal is always to enhance math teaching and learning.

Through our walk-throughs and observations we gain a picture of what is happening within classrooms, but looking at grade-level and schoolwide data allows us a broader view of the math program. Discussing testing data or analyzing student work samples are valuable ways to involve staff in identifying grade-level and schoolwide needs and make program improvement a whole-school process (see Chapter 3). In addition, the needs we identify from classroom observations and school data help us design a professional development plan to bolster our math program (see Chapter 4).

Questions for Reflection

- What classroom comes to mind when I think about good mathematics instruction? What stands out about that classroom?

- What do I frequently see in our mathematics classrooms? Are teachers or students doing most of· the modeling and talking?

- What opportunities do teachers have to examine grade-level standards in adjacent grades?

- What makes a high-quality mathematics activity?

- Do teachers make use of varied levels of questions in our buildings? Are questions used to focus student thinking?

- Is problem solving an integral part of mathematics lessons in our building?

- What conversations do I have with teachers before observations? What questions do I ask?

- Do I look for different things with different teachers? How do I determine what I am looking for with different teachers?

- How do I prepare for the postobservation conference?

- What questions do I ask during the postobservation conference?

    - How do I acknowledge and celebrate what went well?

    - How do I recognize opportunities for growth?

    - How do I communicate recommendations for that growth?

Analyzing Data and Student Work to Gain Insights About Teaching and Learning

We acknowledge that we gain important insights about the effectiveness of our math programs by observing math being taught in classrooms, but in order to construct a comprehensive picture of teaching and learning, we also look at additional data sources. While there are many types of assessment data, we are focusing specifically on two types in this chapter: the analysis of schoolwide assessment data (e.g., national or statewide testing) and the examination of student work samples. While those two types of data are quite different, they both provide invaluable insights into math teaching and learning.

In analyzing testing data, we attempt to make sense of numeric scores. As we support our staffs to work collaboratively to interpret and make sense of the quantitative data, we thrust our teachers into an enormously beneficial reflective experience. Together they identify and celebrate successes as well as pinpoint needs and brainstorm ways to address them. The act of trying to make sense of quantitative scores is an insightful process that requires us to look at what we currently do and decide if it is working or should be adjusted.

In analyzing students' work, we transition from quantitative to qualitative data. The examination of student work is a very different type of data analysis in which we review our students' representations, computations, reasoning, and problem solving. We identify their individual errors and misunderstandings and are able to

45

make specific plans for addressing them. While completely different in scope and detail, both of these examinations of data spur reflection about teaching and learning and help us improve our practice.

Dependent on the district or school, you may also have district benchmark testing or other tests you administer to your students. The protocols discussed next can be modified for other types of data, either quantitative scores or the examination of actual student work. Keep in mind that the focus in this chapter is on *discussing* the scores or work, considering why they look the way they do, and brainstorming ways to improve student learning.

Whether analyzing school testing data or individual student work samples, we look for strengths and needs, consider why the data looks the way it does, and then determine a plan to address what we see. In both cases, it is our thoughtful interpretation of the scores or student work—and our reflections on how they might inform our practice—that are our focus within this chapter.

Analyzing Testing Data

Today's math testing data looks quite different than it did even a few years ago. Math testing data was traditionally reported by math strand, with specific scores for number and operations, geometry, measurement, or data. Today's testing focuses on process as well as content, because our math standards place an emphasis on process skills. Tests assess students' reasoning, communication, problem solving, and representation, but those skills are assessed as they relate to math content. Scores are often reported in categories with merged skills having a single score. When content and process are merged in score reports, it can be difficult for us to figure out exactly what contributed to the number score. And, of course, a number on a score report is not likely to allow us to make direct connections between that score and our math teaching practices. Did the student score low because of content understanding, lack of procedural fluency, problem-solving application, or inability to understand a representation? The scores alone do not clearly indicate what a teacher needs to do to improve learning.

Just as we focus our students on the need to look beyond the answer and explore the meaning of math skills and concepts, we must go beyond the scores on math assessments to figure out why the data looks the way it does. It is up to us to lead thoughtful discussions about these scores to spur insights about teaching and elicit ideas for program improvement. This reflective process helps us conjecture about what we are doing that is working and what aspects of our teaching might need to be adjusted. Analyzing testing data brings all teachers in the school together to make sense of the data and to explore the challenge of improving math teaching and learning.

THE DATA ANALYSIS PROCESS

Looking at assessment reports to identify strengths and needs can be an overwhelming and time-consuming task. In some schools, the initial review of testing data is done by a school committee like the mathematics leadership team or school improvement team, while in others it might be done by grade-level teams or even whole-faculty groups. Team members look for trends, both positive and negative, as they examine the numbers. Which scores look problematic? Which indicate successes? Whether the detailed analysis of the numbers is done by a team or by the whole faculty, everyone should be involved in the subsequent reflections about the data, including special education and intervention teachers, talented and gifted teachers, ELL teachers, and other staff. Some data may be appropriate to discuss with the whole staff, while other data may be more specific to particular grade levels or grade bands.

A PROTOCOL FOR ANALYZING SCHOOL/GRADE DATA

Consider the following possible protocol for examining and analyzing math assessment data with your staff. Keep in mind that test scores do not tell us what is working or not working in our teaching. It is how we analyze the scores, through discussions and reflection, that brings us to important insights about teaching and learning.

1. Teachers first break into small groups to briefly review the scores. Groups are tasked with finding a few successes, a few challenges, a few surprises, and a few "wonders." Teams briefly share their insights about the data.
2. The leadership team, or an administrator, who have already had time to thoroughly review the data, may also share specific data they found to be interesting. Data showing growth or a concern is selected to be the focus for

further teacher reflection. (Note that teachers will likely come up with similar insights when viewing the scores, but the leadership team may have identified some particularly problematic scores and might direct the discussion to begin with those data points.) Because the data itself does not give us specific information on why it looks the way it does, we rely on the teachers to delve into the possible causes, both positive and negative.

3. The small groups then focus on what they believe contributed to the results, being sure to consider different perspectives (e.g., student, staff, school, and curriculum factors, such as those listed in Figure 3.1). This is the critical step of conjecturing why the data looks the way it does. It is teachers who best know what was going on during math instruction. What did they notice about students' skills and prior knowledge? What issues may have surfaced related to time, resources, or curriculum? In what ways did they feel inadequate to handle students' misunderstandings or to address specific standards, possibly needing more support or understanding of the math topic themselves?

4. Teams share their ideas about contributing factors with the larger group, while someone records the ideas.

5. After thoroughly discussing possible contributing factors from all perspectives, the group begins to generate an action plan (more about that later) which addresses ways to improve student achievement from the varied perspectives identified as possible contributing factors. Teacher input here is critical; buy-in is likely to be greater when teachers are involved in suggesting actions and improvements.

Contributing Factors to Consider

Students—What about the students may have contributed to these scores?

- Are there students in the class who lack prerequisite skills and others who already know the skill being taught?

- What specific needs might be causing some students to struggle (e.g., limited language skills for our second-language learners)?

Figure 3.1 Contributing factors to consider

- Are the reading levels of some students impacting their math success?

- Do students have the habits of effective mathematicians (e.g., perseverance, inquiry, collaboration)?

School schedule/environment—What about the school schedule, the classroom math period schedule, or the general school environment may have contributed to the scores?

- Do we have enough instructional time in our math block to accomplish our math goals?

- Is time available to reteach and revisit specific skills and concepts throughout the year?

- Is the math block interrupted by other classes or events throughout the day?

- Are there opportunities for co-teaching for students who have been identified with special needs?

Teachers—What about teachers' knowledge, skills, or attitudes may have contributed to these scores?

- Are there math standards we don't fully understand or may be struggling to teach effectively?

- Do we have difficulty integrating some instructional strategies with specific math content (e.g., math talk, formative assessment, modeling)?

- Do we believe this is an important skill or concept? Are we struggling to help students see its importance?

- Do we believe our students can understand or achieve this? Do we need help finding ways to convince them it is doable?

Curriculum or materials—What about the existing curriculum or available resources may have contributed to these scores?

- Do we have an adequate supply of hands-on materials for students to fully explore the topic?

- Do we have ways for students to visualize the math ideas (e.g., interactive whiteboards, document cameras)?

Figure 3.1 Contributing factors to consider *(cont.)*

- Are there a variety of lesson ideas available to address the skill or topic with different levels of learners?

- Are additional activity or lesson ideas available if we need to extend the time spent on this topic?

- Does the lesson sequence in the curriculum materials match our pacing schedule or is there need to discuss an effective sequence of tasks?

Figure 3.1 Contributing factors to consider *(cont.)*

A Sample Analysis

One school expressed concern about the impact of students' problem-solving skills on some specific scores. The math leadership team shared the scores, as well as some sample test questions, to remind teachers of the types of questions that were a part of the assessment. Teachers briefly discussed the skills needed to be successful with these tasks.

Then, teachers split into grade-level groups with special education and other related teachers joining different teams. Their first task was to brainstorm why the scores were low. To ensure that the teachers did not look at the issue from just one perspective (e.g., focusing on the students' lack of prior knowledge), they were asked to consider the scores from the four perspectives identified in Figure 3.1, recording their ideas for each.

The teachers shared ideas about possible contributing factors related to students' problem solving and then reported their ideas to the whole group. Some of the ideas that emerged follow:

- Students
  - Many students have low reading levels, which impacts their ability to read and comprehend problems.
  - The students have varied ability levels. Some lack the basic computational skills they need. Others just memorized procedures but don't understand when to apply them when solving problems.
  - Students struggle to identify strategies to solve problems.
  - Students give up easily.

- School schedule/environment
  - There is not enough time in math class to routinely teach problem solving.
  - Students are able to solve problems with division or fractions when we are teaching it but then forget it when we move on to another math topic.
- Teachers
  - Teaching computations is easier, but teaching problem solving is hard. We need ideas for how to help students.
- Curriculum or materials
  - Our curriculum has grade-level ideas, but we need to know what to do when students are behind (e.g., students who didn't get a foundation for two-step problems or who don't understand comparison problems even though they were introduced to those skills at an earlier grade).
  - We need more problems that integrate with the content we are teaching.

These discussions moved the teachers from the typical excuses for students' inability to solve the problems, like "They are not reading it carefully," or "They are being lazy," to a more introspective and comprehensive list of possible contributing factors for why these scores may have been low. We'll return to this example, and the suggested actions, when we discuss action plans later.

FOLLOWING UP: MAKING A SCHOOL OR GRADE-LEVEL PLAN

When we are planning changes across a school or grade level, some actions are the responsibility of the school leaders (e.g., scheduling adjustments, coaching opportunities, or resource purchases), while others will be implemented by teachers (e.g., increased focus on math vocabulary, having math tool boxes available in all classrooms). We also need to focus on how to measure the actions and how we will know when they have been successful.

- Meeting notes are given to all staff, highlighting their ideas and plans. The notes can be added as an appendix to the school improvement plan.
- Throughout the year, update meetings are held to discuss actions, check progress, and readjust plans.
- At the end of the year, the data and notes from data discussions are reviewed to update the school improvement plan.

School leaders emerge from these data analysis meetings with "to do" lists as they order supplies, readjust schedules, join collaborative planning meetings, arrange professional learning opportunities, observe classroom teaching, and continue to monitor data. Different grade levels might select different actions/interventions with a few actions common across the school.

A Sample School-Level Plan

Let's return to the school that was working on improving students' problem-solving skills (see page 50). Once teams shared their thoughts on contributing factors, the group split back into grade-level teams to identify possible actions. These ideas were then shared and discussed with the whole group. Some ideas that emerged included the following:

- Students
  - Identify small groups within the classroom to address problem solving at different levels.
  - Identify strategies to teach comprehension of word problems.
    - » Allow students to read problems with partners.
    - » Encourage retelling and summarizing of the problem prior to solving it.
    - » Explore ways to visualize problems to support comprehension, including the use of materials or the drawing of diagrams.
  - Discuss and then post anchor charts with possible problem-solving strategies to support those who may need a review of strategies.
  - Discuss perseverance for those who are quick to give up. Brainstorm strategies to "get unstuck" when solving problems.
- School schedule/environment
  - Explore the possibility of finding more time in the school schedule for math instruction.
  - Look at the math block to see if anything can be eliminated or reduced, allowing more time for problem tasks (e.g., reducing the number of computations done in isolation to allow time for problem-based tasks).
  - Revisit computations through problems throughout the year, maybe designating days in which class problems relate to various math content to be sure we spiral back to past computation skills.

- ⊚ Consider a schoolwide program to create enthusiasm for problem solving (e.g., maybe highlighting one student each week for his or her method or perseverance).
- Teachers
  - ⊚ Explore possible professional learning opportunities related to problem solving (e.g., ideas for modeling problems, exploring two-step problems, focusing on reasonableness, exploring problem structures . . .).
  - ⊚ Write problems together at collaborative planning meetings, and discuss our expectations for student work, then give problems to students and bring papers back to collaborative planning to review and analyze.
  - ⊚ Begin a school or grade-level book study about teaching problem solving.
  - ⊚ Have grade-band discussions about ways in which we explore problem-solving situations at different grade levels.
- Curriculum or materials
  - ⊚ Have meetings with grade-level teachers from the previous year to discuss their math standards related to problem solving and gather ideas for students who have not mastered those prior skills.
  - ⊚ Explore the progression of problem-solving standards K–5 to identify what is new at each grade level and then identify specific lessons to address those new skills.
  - ⊚ Create student toolkits to offer support with computational skills during problem-solving tasks (e.g., multiplication charts, hundred charts, manipulatives, calculators).

The group then considered all of the ideas and chose strategies for inclusion in the school action plan. One particularly important aspect of the plan focused on how teachers might monitor their students' growth in problem solving. They decided to conduct a monthly analysis of a grade-level problem-solving task in order to monitor their students' skills, identify their specific needs, and make necessary teaching adjustments along the way.

While this example cited a focus area (problem solving) that was schoolwide, the same process can be used in grade-level meetings to examine data and develop action plans specific to grade-level concerns. This process is flexible and should be adjusted to meet the needs of your school. The key element is that teachers, with the guidance of administrators and math coaches, play a significant part in identifying why scores might look the way they do and then reflect and brainstorm a doable plan for improving student learning. This process acknowledges that it is unlikely that a single action will significantly impact student achievement, and focuses on looking at the data from multiple perspectives and identifying multiple actions to support students' continued growth.

Analyzing Students' Work

Analyzing our students' work provides us with invaluable insights into their skills and understandings. As teachers, we know what we have taught, but it can be eye-opening to see what our students can actually do when faced with math tasks. This analysis provides specific information about students' math learning that school-wide assessment data cannot provide, and it allows for a more timely response to the needs that are uncovered. Examination of student work helps us pinpoint specific actions and interventions to improve students' learning and allows us to validate or question our own teaching strategies.

Teachers work together in this collaborative process to examine our students' math work, determine strengths and needs, reflect on the causes for their errors, and then discuss implications for instruction and next steps in the classroom. It is formative assessment at its best! The goal is not to score students' work but to learn from it, to see what students can do and then discuss how we can adjust teaching to address their needs.

While school testing data is analyzed once or twice a year, dependent on when scores are released, examination of student work should be done throughout the school year. Many schools have monthly meetings to examine work samples, finding it to be a critical way to identify students' needs and refocus their instructional efforts.

CHOOSING TASKS FOR REVIEW

The best math tasks are ones that require students to apply math skills to solve problems. In these types of tasks, we are able to determine if students can interpret problems and employ strategies to solve them, if they can apply computational

See the online resources for some samples of constructed-response math assessments for grades K–5. These tasks are in Word format so they can be easily modified to meet your needs.

skills as needed, and if they can model, explain, and/or justify their math thinking. Having all students in a particular grade do the same task allows for in-depth discussions about that particular task, although teachers might assign different tasks with a common focus (e.g., different problems but all related to division).

A PROTOCOL FOR DISCUSSION

These meetings are best conducted in grade-level teams, facilitated by a math coach or other school leader or content expert. Using a protocol ensures that teachers are able to move through the process from start to finish, rather than getting stuck on discussing students' errors or misconceptions and leaving no time to brainstorm solutions. Consider the following protocol that guides teachers through the process:

Introduction (2–3 minutes)

- Teachers are introduced to their task—to work together to examine their students' work to answer the following questions:
  - What math skills (computation, problem solving, communication) are strengths for our students? Which are concerns?
  - What instructional strategies might support students in strengthening these skills?

Focusing (5–7 minutes)

- If all teachers had their students do the same math task, the teachers discuss the type of response that would "meet their expectations."
- If the tasks are varied, the teachers briefly describe the specific task they assigned, explaining what they hope to see in students' responses.

Examination of Student Work Samples (15–20 minutes)

- Teachers work with a partner to review and discuss their work samples. They alternate papers between their two classes so each teacher has an opportunity to view their students' work and their partner's students' work.
- Teachers discuss and record observations about what the students were successfully able to do.
- They discuss and record observations about areas of concern. (See Figure 3.2.)

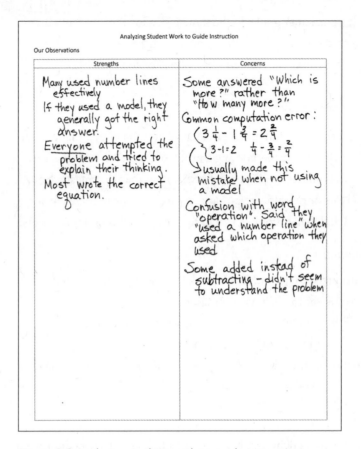

Figure 3.2 Analyzing student work to guide instruction

Group Feedback (10–15 minutes)

- Partners share their observations with a small group of peers. Participants back up comments with specific examples from student work.
  - ◉ Observations about strengths—examples of student successes?
  - ◉ Observations about concerns—gaps, errors, misconceptions?

Implications for Instruction (15–20 minutes)

- Partners discuss what they will do as a result of what they observed. Providing teachers with questions to guide their thinking (see Figure 3.3) leads to more productive discussions:
  - ◉ What will you teach or reteach?

- How will you teach it?
- How will you assess progress?
- Pairs record ideas and insights.

Group Feedback (10–15 minutes)

- Partners share their ideas about instructional implications with the group.
  - How will they address the concerns?
  - What steps will they take?

Reflection (3–5 minutes)

- Teachers quietly reflect on the ideas that they plan to use in their classrooms.
- Teachers are encouraged to record a few ideas for a personal action plan.
  - What will you continue to do?
  - What will you add in your teaching?
  - What will you delete in your teaching?
  - What will you adjust in your teaching?

Implications for Instruction

What will you teach?

- What should be your focus in upcoming lessons?

  - Do your students have adequate foundation skills to solve the problems you are posing?

  - Are students able to select appropriate strategies to solve problems?

  - Are students able to apply their computational skills to solve problems?

  - Are students able to effectively communicate their thinking through words or models?

- Are there any skills that need to be retaught to the whole class or a small group of students?

  - Is there a particular problem-solving strategy that is difficult for your students?

Figure 3.3 Implications for instruction

- Is there a particular step in the problem-solving process that is most challenging for your students (e.g., identifying the question, choosing a strategy, checking answer for reasonableness)?

- Is there a particular computation error or conceptual misunderstanding that is causing incorrect answers?

- Is there a particular communication skill that would support your students in expressing their math ideas?

How will you teach it?

See the online resources for a copy of these questions to distribute to teachers.

- **Are your instructional activities appropriate for your objectives?**

  - What types of classroom activities (e.g., partner work, teacher demonstrations and think alouds, group tasks, hands-on activities) might be helpful in developing the necessary skills?

  - Are you giving students an opportunity to experience mathematics in visual, hands-on, and abstract ways?

  - Are you posing a variety of problem-solving tasks?

  - Are you demonstrating writing skills or offering guided practice with writing tasks?

- **Do the samples suggest the need for differentiating instruction for certain lessons?**

  - Do you notice that some students are struggling with problems that others are easily solving?

  - Do you notice that some students are writing more thoroughly or more effectively than others?

  - How will you meet the needs of your students who are at different skill levels (e.g., flexible grouping, modified assignments, differentiated centers, tutoring, more-challenging tasks)?

Figure 3.3 Implications for instruction *(cont.)*

How will you assess progress?

· How will you evaluate further student progress in your areas of concern?

  · Will you collect and analyze additional work samples following some classroom interventions?

  · Will you modify your assessments to attempt to pinpoint student progress?

  · Will you use alternate assessment strategies (observation, student interviews)?

  · Will you conference with individual students to assess their growth?

Figure 3.3 Implications for instruction *(cont.)*

This protocol brings teachers through the process of observing their students' work, discussing observations with partners and then a small group, and finally brainstorming instructional strategies to address what they have seen in the students' work (see Figure 3.4). The partner work allows for a more intimate discussion, balanced by the small-group discussions in which pairs gain other perspectives and additional ideas. Finally, teachers are asked to reflect on what they will take from the discussions as they record their personal action plans.

When time permits, it is best to look at all student papers, but if time does not permit, teachers should select papers from varied levels of students so they are able to see a range of students' responses to the task. Teachers might also select work of students that are "on their radar" for enrichment or intervention in order to continue to monitor their math work.

This same type of protocol can be used for examining district benchmark tests that contain constructed-response items, with teachers discussing students' strengths and needs and then planning interventions to address them.

Figure 3.4 Teachers work together to examine student work and discuss strategies for improving math teaching and learning.

Tips for Analyzing Student Work

- Remind teachers to be objective—the focus is on the work we see, not on what we think our students can do.
- Select tasks that are problem-based and require students to (1) solve a problem, (2) apply computational skills and conceptual understanding, and (3) communicate about their results.
- Observe for content and process skills. While you are observing for students' multiplication skills, you are also observing their ability to comprehend the problem as well as their skill at justifying their answers.
- Stick to a protocol so you have time to get through the process. There is nothing more discouraging than identifying needs and running out of time before you can identify solutions.
- Link what you have learned about your students to your own teaching. Reflections should consider cause and effect. What have we done to elicit the successes we see? What could we do to cause other students to "get it"?

The process—both in analyzing testing data and reviewing student work—is intended to be a learning experience for teachers but also to transfer to a learning experience for students. For that to happen, we need an action plan based on our analyses.

INDIVIDUAL ACTION PLANS TO IMPROVE STUDENT LEARNING

Through a thoughtful analysis of student work, teachers gain insight into varied ways they can modify their teaching and improve student learning. Teachers should consider reasonable actions based on their students' observed strengths and needs. What skills should be revisited or retaught? Which students would benefit from additional support? In what ways might instruction be modified to improve students' learning? Based on the results of their analysis, they might

- return the papers to students and discuss the task, sharing specific examples of models, equations, or explanations
- review a skill or discuss a common misconception with the whole class
- pull a small group to reteach or extend a skill
- interview a particular student to find out more about his thinking
- reteach and then pose a similar task to look for improvement.

Analyzing students' work is about gaining insights that help us make adjustments in our teaching.

Whether we are analyzing school assessment data or examining individual student work samples, our teachers gather insights about their students' strengths and needs and are better able to design plans for addressing those needs. In many cases, however, our elementary teachers struggle with how to meet their students' needs. Some may lack understanding of specific standards or math content, while others may benefit from additional strategies to build student understanding of math skills and concepts. At a time when standards, curriculum, and teaching strategies are changing, our teachers benefit from ongoing and effective professional learning opportunities. Chapter 4 explores strategies for designing and facilitating high-quality professional learning.

Questions for Reflection

- What data do we review during data conversations?

- How do we structure our data discussions?

- What topics do we target after reviewing data?

- What are the outcomes of our data conversations? What actions do we take?

- How do we discuss progress toward our goals?

- What opportunities does our staff have to discuss student work as a team?

- How can we build time into our schedule to allow for collaborative data discussions?

- How do we select tasks for class- or grade-level data conversations?

Professional Learning to Enhance Math Teaching

Teaching mathematics is a highly skilled craft. It involves listening to students, responding to their thinking, and adjusting our approaches based on students' needs. It requires a deep understanding of math content, standards, student expectations, assessment procedures, and teaching strategies. With the significant number of shifts in recent years in the teaching of mathematics, professional learning is a must. How can teachers be expected to teach to standards that they do not fully understand? How will teachers comprehend our new view of what constitutes math proficiency? How can teachers be supported to identify, understand, adopt, and refine up-to-date instructional practices? We must provide ongoing, focused, and high-quality professional learning experiences for our elementary math teachers. Some professional learning opportunities may be indicated for the entire staff, while others may be specific to grade-level teams or even to a particular group of teachers.

Characteristics of High-Quality Professional Learning

For many of us, the first and only image that comes to mind when considering professional development is faculty workshops. For many teachers, a host of negative memories arise of the whole staff listening to someone tell them about an initiative or strategy, as they struggled to figure out how it applied to them. Many felt they either already knew what was being presented or they simply didn't care about what was being presented. Words like "boring," "useless," and "waste of time" echoed in the halls following the session. Professional development was something done *to* teachers rather than *for* teachers. Our goal is to change that feeling about professional learning, and to do that we have to change the learning itself. Professional learning should be

- needs-based
- motivating
- practical
- research-based
- ongoing
- positive
- interactive
- reflective.

Considering these characteristics as we design opportunities for our staff ensures a higher likelihood that the sessions are productive and well-received and that they ultimately help us meet our math goals.

PROFESSIONAL LEARNING SHOULD BE NEEDS-BASED

Professional learning should be connected to the needs of our teachers and students. As we mentioned in previous chapters, those needs surface as a result of walk-throughs, observations, and our analysis of data and student work. But needs may also surface as we listen to teachers talk about instruction. Conversations during meetings, like collaborative planning meetings, can indicate a need for professional development of specific skills and strategies. Professional development topics that arise as the result of meaningful teacher conversation around student data and instructional practice are often the most appealing for teachers because they were the ones who articulated the need and can envision using the ideas within their classrooms.

Asking teachers to suggest trainings they believe would be beneficial provides us with helpful data. With new curriculum, new resources, and new methodologies, teachers often have concerns, questions, or confusions about how to move forward. Many schools have found teacher self-assessments to be helpful in revealing needs and helping to identify areas in which teachers may feel insecure or unprepared to support their students. Keep in mind, however, that sometimes teachers may be unaware of their needs, either believing they already know what to do or believing the new content or strategies are not relevant to them. Considering their requests for training, but weighing observational data and student achievement data with those requests, helps us select the most appropriate professional learning options. At the least, we can give them choice about topics and formats so that they have input into their professional development.

See the online resources for a sample Teacher Needs Assessment.

Some needs you might discover through this process include the following:

- **helping teachers better understand the standards they teach**
  - ⊚ Do our teachers truly understand what the standards are saying? Do they have a clear picture of the expectations for their students?
  - ⊚ Do they understand the progression of the standards (what students are taught in the grade prior and what they will face in the following grade)?
  - ⊚ Do they understand both content and practice standards and how they are interrelated?
- **strengthening our teachers' content understanding**
  - ⊚ Do our teachers understand the math content they are teaching?
  - ⊚ Do they understand how math topics connect with one another?
  - ⊚ Can they explain why procedures are done in a particular way or how one math skill connects to another? Might teachers need to relearn math content based on understanding rather than memorized procedures?
  - ⊚ Are they aware of common errors and misconceptions related to specific math content?
  - ⊚ Is there a particular math topic that is problematic (e.g., fractions or number sense)?
- **helping our teachers rethink their feelings and beliefs about math**
  - ⊚ Do our teachers have positive views of math?

- Do they need help building their own confidence about and like of math?
- Are they receptive to changing the way they teach math? Do they understand why math teaching needs to change?
- Do they acknowledge the importance of understanding math concepts and skills, as well as the limitations of teaching math through memorized procedures?
- Do our teachers believe that all students can learn? Does their teaching show recognition of and attention to this belief?

- **assisting our teachers in discovering instructional strategies and assessment techniques to effectively meet their goals**
  - Can they identify teaching practices that build students' process skills including reasoning, communication, representation, and problem solving?
  - Have teachers tried these instructional strategies? Have their attempts been successful, or do they need additional support? Where are they in the process of implementing new teaching strategies?
  - Do they plan intentional, coherent mathematics lessons and activities that incorporate these strategies?
  - Do our teachers know what math proficiency looks like for an elementary-level student? Do they know how to identify when students are, or are not, proficient? Do they need support in assessing students' math proficiency?
  - Do they know how to identify students who struggle with particular skills and concepts or students who would benefit from enrichment? Do they know how to modify tasks and instruction to support those students?

See the Thinking Through a Lesson feature in each module of the Math in Practice grade-level books for examples of blending practical ideas and critical reflections about teaching. These lessons are coupled with the important instructional decisions teachers make as they conduct the lesson, ensuring that teachers see beyond the simple activity ideas.

Your answers to these questions can identify your staff's needs and guide your decisions about the professional learning options that make the most sense in your school or district.

PROFESSIONAL LEARNING SHOULD BE MOTIVATING, PRACTICAL, AND GROUNDED IN RESEARCH

Professional learners are motivated when the information presented is seen as useful to their teaching and to their students' learning. Many professional learning sessions disseminate activities (which teachers do appreciate) but fail to increase teachers' math understanding and skills. While practical activities are great, the session must extend beyond practical activities to ensure that teachers understand why those activities make sense, how they were developed, and the best ways to implement them to promote learning. Knowing the research that underlies effective classroom activities—for example, how modeling supports students' math understanding—enables a teacher to move beyond a specific activity in which students create models for fractions and allows them to apply this theory to their work using models with other math skills and concepts.

PROFESSIONAL LEARNING SHOULD BE ONGOING AND POSITIVE

Professional learning should not leave a teacher feeling overwhelmed or incompetent. The message should be clear that this is something teachers can do and that they will be given support as they implement the ideas. There should be opportunities for teachers to try approaches with their students and then revisit the strategies, discussing their successes and failures as they work to expand their teaching approaches.

High-quality professional learning provides teachers with a series of interrelated opportunities to extend and deepen their understanding over time. A full faculty workshop to introduce certain strategies might be followed by grade-level meetings in which teachers discuss the strategies specific to their students and then collaboratively plan lessons to implement them in their classrooms. Having an experienced math coach provide further support through co-teaching or observing some teachers, in a nonevaluative manner, is another way to boost implementation of the strategies. We know that when teachers try to implement new approaches, they often abandon their attempts if they don't see results quickly. We foster perseverance when we provide them with ongoing professional development, time to refine their skills, and colleagues to support them through the process.

PROFESSIONAL LEARNING SHOULD BE INTERACTIVE AND REFLECTIVE

Rather than being talked to, high-quality professional learning allows teachers to share their experiences and insights. They are an active part of the learning experience. This does not mean that teachers need to be doing math activities for all of every session. While engagement in hands-on learning is wonderful (see Figure 4.1), active involvement can also come in the form of talk between teachers. Asking teachers

Figure 4.1 Professional learning should be positive, interactive, and reflective as teachers identify, explore, analyze, and reflect on strategies to support student learning.

to reflect on the activities helps them think through what makes a particular lesson effective, what changes in questioning might elicit deeper learning, what hands-on experiences might offer opportunities for formative assessment, or what teaching adjustments might benefit particular groups of students. They become active learners, reflecting on their teaching practice and considering the impact of their teaching on students' learning. Reflection is a critical component of all professional learning.

Exploring Professional Learning Options

Planning professional learning based on the needs of our schools, teachers, and students involves orchestrating a series of opportunities for teachers to be introduced to ideas, reflect on those ideas, try to implement them, and continue to refine and extend their skills. This is not done in one session or with one format. While multiple types of experiences are involved, they are woven together by the big ideas being addressed. And we follow, modify, and evaluate the learning throughout the year.

Options for professional learning might include faculty groups like collaborative planning meetings, book study groups, or lesson study. They might be coaching opportunities like co-teaching or demonstration lessons. They may be workshops or a variety of other brief opportunities for quick reflections about teaching and learning. Consider weaving together some of these options as you design a comprehensive professional learning program for your staff.

PROFESSIONAL LEARNING THROUGH COLLABORATIVE MEETINGS

With our understanding that professional learning happens when we reflect on our teaching and our students' learning, emphasizing collaborative formats just makes sense. Professional learning communities (PLCs) are now a routine part of school cultures. A PLC is a group of educators who meet regularly, share their own expertise, consider students' learning, and ultimately collaborate on improving teaching and learning. Not every faculty group is a PLC. Grade-level meetings that are focused on scheduling field trips or faculty meetings to go over the book fair schedule are not PLCs. PLCs engage teachers in opportunities to discuss teaching and learning with their peers.

PLCs come in a variety of shapes and sizes. They might be required of all staff, being the main component of the professional development plan, or they might be optional, providing opportunities for interested teachers to expand their knowledge and skills. They can be grade-level specific or have representatives across all grades, as well as special educators, ELL teachers, music, P.E., art, or other teachers. They can occur during the school day or after hours.

Math PLC meetings can take various formats.

- Collaborative planning meetings provide a forum for teachers to discuss grade-level math standards, co-plan lessons, discuss pacing, examine student work, and gather insights about math teaching.
- Book study groups are a simple and engaging way to get teachers reading and responding to professional literature about important topics in math teaching and learning.
- Lesson study involves teachers co-planning a math lesson, observing one teacher conducting the lesson, and then evaluating the lesson together.

- Inquiry groups focus on readings and discussions related to a critical teaching question. Some inquiry groups go a step further and become action research groups in which teachers engage in research in their own classrooms related to that question. They try a technique or strategy with their students, gather observations and data on the results, and draw conclusions about teaching issues, sharing their observations and insights with colleagues in the group.

In each of these group formats, teachers have an ongoing opportunity to reflect on teaching and learning with their peers. See the chart in Figure 4.2 for a brief overview of different types of faculty groups, including the purpose of the group, the possible roles of the leader, and some special considerations for each type.

Type of Group	Purpose of Group	Possible Roles of the Leader	Comments/ Considerations
Grade Level Collaborative Planning Meetings	• To co-plan lessons or units • To share ideas/activities related to specific math standards • To subgroup students for specific lessons or skills • To ensure that teachers are following curriculum pacing guidelines • To help teachers on a specific grade level coordinate their pacing • To ensure that standards are appropriately addressed	• Develop a meeting agenda to guide discussions. • Provide guidance on math curriculum/standards issues. • Have math standards and curriculum guides available at all times for reference. • Share pacing guidelines. • Share strategies to help teachers align their class' pacing with suggested pacing guidelines. • Share ideas for addressing standards. • Maintain meeting notes.	• Balance the sharing of information by leader and participants. • Important to develop a "team" atmosphere. • Important to set a clear agenda and monitor time so all tasks are addressed. • Insight from these meetings will help you identify teachers who may need individual support.

Figure 4.2 A look at faculty groups

Type of Group	Purpose of Group	Possible Roles of the Leader	Comments/ Considerations
Student Work Analysis Meetings (may or may not be a part of collaborative planning)	• To provide teachers with opportunities to analyze samples of their students' work • To promote reflection about teaching based on a look at student work • To help teachers develop insights based on student performance (work samples) • To revisit lessons based on insights gathered	• Help teachers decide on the type of student work that should be brought to the meeting. • Facilitate the discussions by following a protocol. • Prompt teacher reflection and help develop an action plan based on observations/insights. • Summarize key ideas/ insights.	• Time can be a factor when analyzing student work so stick to a schedule. • May need to streamline the process by having teachers bring selected work samples to the meeting (e.g. 5–7 samples from students functioning above, below, and on grade level).
Meetings to Address Specific Student Concerns (may or may not be a part of collaborative planning)	• To discuss concerns related to individual students' math learning • To brainstorm possible interventions to strengthen a student's math understanding	• Listen to concerns/ask questions to gather data. • Volunteer to observe the student during class or conduct some diagnostic tests to gather additional data. • Suggest possible classroom interventions.	• Prior to the meeting, gather any available testing data and bring it to the meeting. • Keep the meeting focused on an action plan. (e.g., What can the team do to support this student?) • Be sure the action plan includes a date to revisit the concerns.
Book Study Groups	• To provide an ongoing professional development opportunity for teachers based on the strategies and ideas in a professional book • To promote teacher reflection	• Participate in the selection of the book (it may be selected by the administrator or coach based on school needs— or—some book choices may be presented to teachers)	• Select a book that will motivate teachers and extend their professional knowledge. • Remind teachers of upcoming meetings so they are prepared (e.g., have read the chapter).

Figure 4.2 A look at faculty groups *(cont.)*

Type of Group	Purpose of Group	Possible Roles of the Leader	Comments/ Considerations
Book Study Groups *(Cont.)*	• To promote collegiality • To prompt implementation of new strategies within classrooms	• Organize the ongoing meeting schedule • Facilitate discussions at sessions • Provide feedback sheets or implementation ideas for between sessions	• Make assignments doable (e.g., read a chapter vs. a whole book). • If done after school hours, look for ways to motivate teachers (e.g. stipend money, snacks, providing an enjoyable experience).
Lesson Study Groups	• To promote reflection about lesson planning and delivery through team planning and teaching experiences • To promote collegiality • To increase teachers' skills at planning and delivering effective lessons • To promote in-depth exploration of a particular math teaching topic	• Develop a schedule for team planning, observation, and analysis of the lesson. • Participate in the planning and analysis discussions. • Find coverage so teachers can view the lesson they helped to plan. • Guide the lesson analysis.	• Work with teams to select a standard/objective for a lesson well in advance, so teams have adequate time to research, plan, and discuss their lesson ideas. • If it is impossible to cover classes so all teachers on the team can view the delivery of the lesson, consider videotaping it so they can all see it.
Inquiry/Action Research Groups	• To promote reflection related to a specific question that is important to the school or grade level (e.g., In what ways can we help strengthen our students' abilities to write about their math understanding?) • To provide an ongoing professional development opportunity in which teachers explore their own teaching	• Guide participants in the development of a critical question • Gather articles for teachers to read as they explore and discuss the topic • Facilitate the group discussions • Develop a schedule for ongoing meetings.	• Facilitators must be well prepared to facilitate these discussions. This might require gathering reading material or preparing discussion questions that spark teacher conversation. • For action research: Seeing data from their own classrooms can be a powerful tool for reflection.

Figure 4.2 A look at faculty groups *(cont.)*

Type of Group	Purpose of Group	Possible Roles of the Leader	Comments/ Considerations
Inquiry/Action Research Groups *(Cont.)*	• For action research groups: to gather classroom data related to the critical question and to promote reflection about teaching and learning based on that data	• For action research: share possible research methods and support teachers as they gather and analyze data	• Gathering data can be time-consuming and the research component can be intimidating for some teachers

Figure 4.2 A look at faculty groups *(cont.)*

Collaborative Planning Meetings

Collaborative planning meetings focus on discussing and reflecting on the day-to-day aspects of teaching math. During these meetings, grade-level teachers meet to discuss their current math standards and teaching. Special education teachers or interventionists working with their students are a part of the meetings. During these meetings, led by the school administrator, math coach, or team leader, teachers discuss their plans for addressing upcoming math standards, discussing student expectations, sharing lesson ideas, identifying resources, discussing common math misconceptions, and designing formative assessment tasks. Teachers might discuss specific students, share ideas for intervention or enrichment, and develop strategies to modify tasks or instruction for those students. These sessions are much more than simply sharing activities connected to upcoming content.

When time allows, student work from previous math lessons might be examined to ascertain what to do next to improve student learning (see Chapter 3). In many cases, these meetings are simply not long enough to achieve all of these goals, so pacing meetings or meetings to analyze student work may be scheduled at separate times. However, each of those tasks is critical and must happen on a regular basis throughout the year. Many schools have designed their schedules to allow for weekly collaborative planning time while other schools may schedule these meetings every other week. Finding the time for the meetings and facilitating the meetings to make the best use of the allotted time ensure the success of these critical opportunities for discussions and reflection among teachers.

Faculty Study Groups

Professional study groups like book study groups, lesson study, or inquiry or action research groups are more general in scope, less focused on tomorrow's lesson, and more focused on the study of and reflection about math teaching as a whole. The topics might arise from school-improvement initiatives, insights from walk-throughs or classroom observations, or simply topics selected by teachers that focus on matters they want to know more about. These topics can be general or quite specific.

- What significant changes should be made in math teaching? Where do we begin?
- How do we integrate the standards for mathematical practice into our daily teaching?
- How can we support students becoming more effective math problem solvers?
- How do we get students to better retain math skills and concepts?
- What changes to our questioning will lead to better student understanding?
- How do we do a better job at integrating technology into our math lessons?
- How can we support increased achievement by our ELL students?

If teachers have not had experience as members of study groups, it is important to begin with clear expectations of what a study group is and what it is not. Consider the following:

A study group is not . . .	A study group is . . .
. . . an unfocused chat session.	. . . a group of professionals discussing issues related to a specific aspect of their work.
. . . a gripe session.	. . . a group of professionals who acknowledge struggles but search for answers together.
. . . a workshop in which one person presents information.	. . . a group of professionals sharing their experiences and knowledge.
. . . just a session to *talk* about instruction.	. . . a forum to make changes in group members' instructional practices.
. . . a place to discuss what we cannot accomplish.	. . . a place to discuss what we can accomplish and how we can accomplish it.

Members of study groups are not passive learners. An important activity in the initial meeting is setting expectations for participation. Asking participants to discuss their role, and what they need to do to ensure the success of the group, gives them ownership and helps prevent the often-seen dilemma of participants sitting quietly, waiting for the leader to disseminate information to them. With some support, participants are likely to determine their responsibilities to be similar to the following:

- attend all sessions and participate in discussions
- share "tips" or activities they have tried
- ask questions about things they are concerned about
- bring related resources, strategies, or readings to the meetings to share with the group
- be open to new ideas and try ideas and strategies between group meetings.

In faculty study groups, facilitators might plan an activity, pose a question, or suggest a reading to initiate the conversation, ask questions to prompt or refocus discussions, and pose a question or task at the end of the meeting to keep teachers thinking/involved between sessions. Let's consider specific roles, structures, and benefits for two types of faculty study groups—book study and lesson study.

PROFESSIONAL BOOK STUDY

A wealth of professional literature explains and illustrates high-quality math teaching, but with planning lessons, grading papers, maintaining their classrooms, communicating with parents, and the many other tasks that teachers perform each day, when do they find the time for professional reading? Book study groups can be a great way to introduce teachers to enlightening professional books that strengthen their understanding of math content and pedagogy and have the added benefit of encouraging reflection about teaching.

As teachers read the chosen book, they gather instructional ideas and encounter differing perspectives on teaching. Meetings become the time to discuss, debate, and reflect on the ideas. The format respects teachers' knowledge and insights and challenges them to discuss what they have read, examine the ideas, and select those that they want to try with students. Through the selection of just the right book, the careful pacing of the reading assignments to make it doable for teachers' busy schedules, and skilled leadership during book study meetings, this format provides both information and reflection about teaching and learning.

While some schools have organized book study as an optional, after-school study group, others have made it their preferred professional development format, with all teachers participating in a book study with meetings scheduled monthly or quarterly during professional learning times. In some districts, book study groups allow for cross-school collaboration with teachers moving between schools to join groups with teachers from other elementary buildings.

Books can be selected based on school or district initiatives or can be chosen by the teachers themselves. It is best to give teachers some choice, possibly identifying two or three high-quality books and either allowing teachers to decide which one will be used for the book study or forming a book study group for each book and allowing teachers to select which group they want to join.

The initial meeting of a book study group might consist of paging through the book, exploring the table of contents, setting a schedule for reading, and generating goals for what teachers are hoping to gain from the readings and discussions. In addition, this meeting allows time for discussions about the group norms or expectations for participants' behaviors and contributions. See Figure 4.3 for an example of a completed Goals and Commitments sheet.

A copy of this book study Goals and Commitments form can be found in the online resources.

The success of book study groups depends on teachers reading the assigned selections and being ready and willing to share their reflections about the reading. Brief reading selections (e.g., one chapter) generally offer many opportunities for reflection, while asking teachers to read several chapters may frustrate them and undermine the progress of the group. Skipping some book chapters, dependent on the needs and interests of group members, is okay. Once teachers become engaged with a book, they often go back and read the skipped chapters on their own. That is one of the greatest advantages of book study: Teachers are enticed into reading books they might not otherwise have taken the time to read. By offering short, manageable chunks of reading and engaging follow-up discussions, these groups demonstrate to teachers that professional reading is both beneficial and doable.

The sample Book Study Reflection sheets in Figure 4.4 are available in the online resources.

Many facilitators find that reflection sheets encourage teachers to complete the reading and help them identify a few key points to share during the group meeting (see Figure 4.4). These forms are brief, to respect teachers' time, but they do ask teachers to jot down specific insights to ensure that discussions at the meetings are productive. Consider the possibilities in Figure 4.4, in which teachers make brief notes about their reading or jot down quotes to be discussed with colleagues.

Book Title—*Math in Practice: A Guide for Teachers*
Members: Sue O., John S. Marcy M., Laura H., Allison P., Cheryl A., Kay S., Joan T.

Our Goals:

- to explore changes in math teaching
- to identify teaching practices that promote math understanding
- to gather strategies/activities for teaching problem solving
- to try new techniques with our students
- to think about our own teaching
- to gather ideas from each other.

In order to accomplish our goals, we will . . .

. . . be prepared for each session.

- Read the assigned pages before the session.
- Record some reflections to bring to each session.
- Try techniques with our students between sessions.

. . . attend all sessions.

- Be on time, and stay the whole time.
- Turn off cell phones.
- Stay tuned in to the discussions.

. . . actively participate.

- Share our ideas.
- Listen to each other.
- Be prepared to back up our ideas with examples, explanations, or justifications.

. . . be open-minded and respectful.

- Consider different ideas, teaching strategies, and opinions.
- Accept everyone's ideas without judgment.
- Feel free to disagree respectfully.
- Focus discussions on the ideas and not the person who shared them.

Figure 4.3 Sample goals and commitments for a book study group

Book Study Reflection Sheet

Title _____ Chapter _____

Quote from Text	My Thinking About the Quote (Insight? Question?)

Book Study Reflection Sheet

Title _____ Chapter _____

An Important Idea from the Chapter	My Thoughts About It
A related activity/strategy I am going to try	

Book Study Reflection Sheet

Title _____ Chapter _____

Complete at least 3 of the 4 prompts below.

I agree that…
I disagree that…
I am going to try…
A new insight I had…

Book Study Reflection Sheet

Title _____ Chapter _____

3 Strategies/Activities I Want to Try
2 Ideas That Reminded Me of My Students
1 Quote That Got Me Thinking

Figure 4.4 Book study reflection sheets

This Math in Practice series is designed to allow you to capitalize on this professional learning option. *Math in Practice: A Guide for Teachers* shares teaching strategies and is accompanied by study-group questions for ease in facilitating discussions about the ideas. The chapters are easy to read but provide lots to think about related to both math content and teaching strategies.

LESSON STUDY

Lesson study is a professional development format that has been widely used in Japan and has gained popularity in recent years in the United States. Through lesson study, teams of teachers work together to plan, observe, analyze, and revise math lessons, expanding their understanding of math teaching and learning throughout the process.

Team members discuss goals for student learning and then research strategies and collaboratively plan a math lesson based on their goals. Planning the lesson collaboratively allows teachers to discuss lesson ideas using both the research they have done and their own ideas, insights, and experiences. One team member then conducts the lesson, while the others watch and record observations. The team then meets to discuss their observations and use their notes and insights to revise the lesson. In addition, they draw conclusions about student learning and the effectiveness of instructional techniques to apply to future lessons. Some teams then teach the lesson in another classroom and again observe to determine its effectiveness and the effectiveness of their revisions. Figure 4.5 lists the stages of a lesson study.

The power of lesson study is in the collaborative planning and reflection. Teachers work together to better understand and refine their teaching practice. This work is nonthreatening because the lesson is co-planned, and everyone had a hand in its design. It promotes reflection on teaching practices as team members discuss student responses and examine the student data they collect. Lesson study is not effective without time for collaborative planning and reflection and requires creative scheduling, or classroom coverage, to allow all team members to observe the lesson. But when done effectively, lesson study is a powerful professional learning option.

You will find these questions at the end of each chapter in Math in Practice: A Guide for Teachers.

Team Planning and Goal Setting

The team discusses the math standard and researches possible instructional strategies. They work together to plan a math lesson to support the standard.

What do we want students to know or be able to do?

How might we design a lesson to achieve these goals?

What high-quality task will we use to teach the mathematics?

What strategies might students use?

What misconceptions might students have?

Conducting the Lesson

One member conducts the lesson, and the others observe and record.

What are we seeing and hearing that shows evidence of student learning?

How are students responding to the lesson?

What aspects of the lesson are going well and what needs to be rethought?

What purposeful questions did the teacher ask?

What opportunities did students have to share their thinking?

Lesson Debriefing and Discussion

The team discusses their notes following the lesson.

What did we see or hear that was expected? What evidence do we have to determine if students achieved the goal?

What would we do differently next time? Why? What would we expect to see as a result of the changes?

Possibly refine and reteach the lesson.

Lesson Summary

The team summarizes their learning.

What did we learn about math teaching and learning?

Figure 4.5 Stages of lesson study

PROFESSIONAL LEARNING THROUGH MATH COACHING

Not all schools have the benefit of a math coach, but for those that do, professional learning extends far beyond workshops or collaborative planning meetings. The knowledge and skills teachers acquire in these sessions can be extended through coaching experiences in the classroom. Through demonstration lessons, co-teaching opportunities, coaching observations, and one-on-one support, teachers are able to explore and refine new skills. For those schools without a math coach, a district math specialist may be available to provide this type of classroom support, or a more experienced "buddy" teacher may be identified to provide a modified level of support.

Demonstration Lessons

In demonstration lessons, the coach, or teacher, conducts a lesson for others to observe. It is designed to specifically show a strategy or illustrate a standard and is meant to jump-start reflection about the issue being addressed. Often this is done in a teacher's classroom so the teacher can see the reaction of her own students, or it might be done with several teachers watching a lesson in one of their classrooms.

Many teachers are reluctant or anxious about being observed by the math coach, but they are often very willing to allow the coach to come in to their room and conduct a lesson. This allows the coach to "get her foot in the door" to begin discussions about teaching and learning. Demonstration lessons allow a teacher to see teaching in action with her own students (see Figure 4.6). When observing in other classrooms, teachers may contend that strategies won't work with their students, but seeing your own students respond to techniques may be hard to argue with. It is not important that demonstration lessons are perfect; in fact, reflection often occurs when students respond differently than expected or when a question or activity fails to yield the results hoped for. The goal of demonstration lessons is to open discussions. Considering ways to modify the task or teaching to get better results is a productive conversation.

Figure 4.6 Teachers benefit from observing demonstration lessons in their own classrooms with their own students.

Demonstration lessons are successful only if they are meaningful and directed toward a specific goal. Prior to the demonstration, the coach should talk with the teacher about the focus of the lesson, which might have been initiated by the coach or the teacher. During the lesson, the observing teacher should know specifically what she is observing for, and, following the lesson, reflective discussions are critical to be sure that the observing teacher recognized the coach's teaching moves and saw the impact of those moves on student learning.

While demonstration lessons can be eye-opening for teachers and prompt thoughtful discussions, there are some common pitfalls to be aware of. Some of these pitfalls are summarized in Figure 4.7.

Demonstration lessons are fairly nonthreatening for teachers, because they are observing rather than teaching. Demonstrations allow the coach to get into the room, share strategies, and open a conversation about teaching, but they certainly have limitations. Teachers do not learn to incorporate new techniques into their repertoire simply by watching others; they need opportunities to try the techniques with their students. Co-planning and co-teaching lessons can provide guided opportunities for teachers to implement strategies within their own classrooms.

Common Pitfall	Tip for Minimizing It
1. There is no buy-in from the observing teacher. At times, the demonstration lesson is initiated by the school leader or math coach, and the teacher doesn't really want to be observing a lesson.	• Keep the tone relaxed and nonevaluative. • Ask the teacher's input. (What would you like to see from your students? What are your students struggling with? What are you struggling with?)
2. The observing teacher is not watching your lesson. The observing teacher might see this as an opportunity to grade papers or is simply distracted as you teach, not really focusing on the lesson.	• Set expectations for the observer. (What do you want them to be doing during the lesson? Should they be helping? What are they observing? Should they be doing other classroom tasks?) • Focus the observer with some guiding questions. (What do you want them to notice? Groupings? Teacher questioning? Management of manipulatives? Pacing of lesson?) • Briefly explain the lesson objectives and activities prior to delivering the lesson. • Provide the observer with copies of any worksheets or materials given to students.
3. The observing teacher does not notice what you want him to notice. While you have planned the lesson to intentionally show specific techniques, the teacher may simply miss some of the strategies you felt were most important to demonstrate.	• Keep the lesson simple. Design a lesson that will not intimidate but is solid and focused on your goals. The more bells and whistles in the lesson, the more distracted a teacher can be from the intended goal of the demonstration. • Decide what you want the teacher to observe, and be sure it is clear within your lesson.
4. The observing teacher does not know how to integrate the ideas into other lessons. While the teacher may have liked what you demonstrated in that specific lesson, they may be unable to see how those techniques can be transferred to other lessons.	• Have a postdemonstration conference to discuss the strategies you used, your observations of students, and so on. Brainstorm ways for the teacher to integrate the ideas into their teaching. • Select a different math topic/standard, and discuss how to apply the strategies to a lesson focused on that standard. • Offer to co-plan and co-teach the next lesson, giving the teacher more responsibility for planning and delivery.

Figure 4.7 Common demonstration lesson pitfalls

Common Pitfall	Tip for Minimizing It
5. The observing teacher does not reflect on cause/effect. While the teacher may notice that students were engaged or that they got the math idea, she does not make the connection that it was what you did that engaged them or helped them get the big idea.	• Have specific conversations focused on making connections between the teaching strategies and the student behaviors and responses. • Have the teacher tell you positive things she observed about the students, and then ask if she can identify why they may have happened. If student responses were different than she has seen in the past, ask her what may have contributed to that.
6. The lesson goes poorly because you aren't familiar with the students' prior knowledge or the classroom behavior-management routines.	• Visit the classroom prior to the demonstration lesson to observe the teacher's behavior management routines. • Plan the demonstration lesson with the teacher, or share your plan prior to the lesson, allowing her to provide insight into students' current understandings or her classroom routines. • Arrange for the observing teacher to observe math lessons in other classrooms, accompanying her so you can point out specific teacher moves and discuss the lesson following the observation.

Figure 4.7 Common demonstration lesson pitfalls *(cont.)*

Co-Planning and Co-Teaching

The co-teaching model affords teachers an opportunity to learn with a math coach or experienced math teacher. Co-teaching is the process of working collaboratively to plan, deliver, and assess a math lesson or series of lessons. It is an effective coaching strategy for addressing specific teacher concerns ("I am struggling with teaching equivalent fractions to my students."), for supporting teachers with new techniques (e.g., managing the use of manipulatives), or simply providing the opportunity for collaboration and reflection about teaching.

Co-teaching shows that the math coach is willing to roll up her sleeves and work side by side with the teacher. The dialogue during the planning and reflection stages is critical to the success of co-teaching. Following are some helpful guidelines for co-teaching discussions with teachers:

1. Co-planning
   - What will be the lesson objective? (Review math standards and pacing guides to determine the objective. Consider both content and process standards.)
   - How will we know students have achieved our objective? Will we observe their work, listen to their responses, have them do several computations, or have them explain how they do a computation?
   - What instructional activities will help get them there?
   - Which instructional formats will work best (e.g., whole-class, partners, collaborative groups, centers, small teacher-led groups)?
   - What key questions will guide students to understanding?
2. Lesson delivery
   - Who does what? Co-teaching means that both teachers share the teaching responsibilities. Be sure that the teacher knows that he will be doing part of the teaching and which part of the teaching that will be.
   - Initially, you might volunteer to do lesson components that may be intimidating for the teacher, giving him an opportunity to see your teaching strategies.
3. Lesson reflection
   - Discuss the lesson assessment. If it is written, review it together, and discuss students' mastery of the objective. If you chose to assess through teacher observations, discuss your observations.
   - What were students able to do as a result of the lesson?
   - In what areas will they need more help?
   - How did the decisions you made during the lesson planning lead to the results you observed? What worked? What would you do differently next time?
   - Discuss possible next steps and/or a plan for the next lesson.

Having the math coach, or expert teacher, roll up her sleeves and engage in the real work of teaching not only supports your teacher's learning but also provides the math coach with powerful information that can inform future professional development decisions. Observations are great "next steps" in a coaching plan (e.g., "Why don't I stop by tomorrow and observe the students as you teach, and we can talk about it after?"). These observations are not evaluative in nature but simply opportunities to provide further coaching and support. For more ideas on observation strategies, see Chapter 2.

Tips for Working with Resistant Teachers

Coaching is about helping teachers change, but not all teachers want to change. It takes a great deal of self-confidence to coach teachers who do not want to be coached. How a school leader or math coach deals with teachers who decline help, are reluctant to accept new ideas, or are sensitive to criticism can be tricky. Consider these ways to help smooth the path to change:

1. Develop a relationship with the teacher. Just as students work harder when they know a teacher cares for them, teachers work harder when they have respect for the math coach or leader and know he has their best interests at heart.

2. Involve the teacher in identifying problems. Allow her to tell you what she is struggling with when teaching math. When needed, show her objective data (e.g., testing data or student work) to help her realize the need. Work to include her in the problem-solving process. Show that you will work with her to help solve the problem. Rather than "You will . . . ", consider "What if we . . . ?"

3. Praise the teacher's positive actions. When negative behaviors need to be addressed, be firm but respectful.

4. Let the teacher talk, rather than jumping in with your answer. Listen, and then suggest ideas (Maybe we could try . . .).

5. Resistance to coaching is often not about the ideas at all but about the fear of change (see Chapter 1). For some teachers, ongoing support and many opportunities to better understand and embrace the change are needed. Provide doable steps. While we may want change to happen overnight, change is more likely if we break it into smaller steps.

6. Do not reference what other teachers do (i.e., Miss Smith starts her lessons with . . .). It is best not to pit teachers against each other. The more general, "some teachers have tried . . ." may be more effective.

7. Find ways to help the teacher see and reflect on his teaching.
   - Talk about cause/effect ("You did . . . , the students did . . ."). Keep discussions objective rather than judgmental.
   - Video-record a lesson, and allow the teacher to see himself teaching.

- Offer to demonstrate, and then co-plan or co-teach with him.
8. Focus on the students and their learning.
   - Make the need for change about what is best for students.
   - Use data to support the need for change (e.g., student work, test scores, student behavior).
9. Allow the teacher to observe effective teaching.
   - Conduct demonstration lessons.
   - Set up a visit to a peer's classroom (and accompany the teacher so you can point out key strategies).
   - Allow the teacher to watch a video of teaching and then discuss the strategies seen.
10. Spend time in the classrooms of effective teachers so that work with a math coach doesn't imply that a teacher is ineffective.
11. Build relationships with teacher leaders in the building so that they are advocates for your coaching efforts.
12. Be approachable and willing to help with any task that makes the teacher more effective as a math teacher.

The school leader and math coach form a strong and collaborative team. Regular discussions between the school leader and the math coach help to refocus efforts when coaching hits snags. The math coach keeps the administrator informed of coaching efforts, particularly when working with resistant teachers. Some ideas for documenting coaching efforts include logs of dates, times, and interventions, notes from observations, and summaries of conferences with the teacher. This information keeps the school leader apprised of what has been tried and helps her determine additional ways to support the teacher.

PROFESSIONAL LEARNING THROUGH WORKSHOPS

Workshops for the full K–5 staff, or for grade bands (e.g., K–2 and 3–5) or grade levels, have a definite place in our professional development plan. Through a workshop format, we can reach a large number of teachers in a short amount of time. We can have discussions and gain insights across grade levels. While we tend to conjure a picture of a speaker in front of the room, disseminating information to the group, workshops can and should be interactive experiences, with frequent partner sharing or collaborative tasks. And as in all professional learning, reflection is essential.

Unfortunately, due to their past experiences, many teachers have developed negative attitudes about workshops. We have all been there—workshops that were a waste of our time! Was it because we had already heard the message multiple times? Was the facilitator dry and unengaging, sharing facts and research but not making them applicable to us or our students? The energy in the room was low, teachers were distracted, and learning was not happening. On the other hand, we have all been in workshops with dynamic presenters who shared activity after activity with engaging jokes and anecdotes. Energy was high and teachers loved it, but we were left thinking: What were the big math ideas? How did the ideas tie together? What were teachers supposed to take away from the session except activities?

Our goal is to engage and energize teachers and leave them with big ideas that change their teaching. How do we balance the practical with the important underlying ideas? How do we design learning sessions in which learning takes place with energy, positivity, and interaction? If the warm-up to share your "favorite math moment" takes half of the session time, will we get to the important ideas and gain the results we hope for? But if the session is a laundry list of "to-dos" and research, will our teachers even tune in long enough to gain insights? Whether you rely on an expert math teacher, a math coach, a district math specialist, or a math expert from outside your district, the goal is to help teachers both understand why the strategies work and gain practical tools to implement them in their classrooms.

Planning Workshops

Professional learning is too important to our teachers and our students' success not to take the time to design sessions thoroughly and intentionally. The workshop itself should be planned beginning with the end in mind—what do we hope to achieve during this session? Pinpointing the goals for the session helps us identify appropriate activities, materials, and time frames. Consider the planning notes in Figure 4.8 to guide your decisions as you plan sessions.

While we want to thoroughly plan the workshop session, it is also important to think about how this session fits into the broader professional development plan for the school or district. Is it an introductory session with a goal of motivating teachers and helping them see the need for a specific initiative? Is it a midpoint session to build on previous sessions, adding new strategies or offering opportunities to share classroom experiences or re-evaluate implementation? Is it a culminating session, to pull together important ideas and strategies across grade levels?

Workshop Planning Notes

Goals for Workshop Participants	Goals for Students
The Workshop Logistics (Location/room setup/materials)	Schedule (Breakdown of topics)
Collaborative Activities (Actively engaging participants)	Reflective Questions (Questions for teachers to discuss)
Feedback (From participants and administrators)	Next Steps (Maintaining the momentum)

Full-size templates for these notes are available in the online resources.

Figure 4.8 Workshop planning notes

Blending Content and Practice

Math professional development sessions should provide content understanding as well as instructional practices. If a session is focused on math content (e.g., adding fractions with like denominators), that content should be presented in such a way as to incorporate the strategies and resources to be used in the classroom when teaching that content. Providing content-specific professional development that does not employ instructional strategies makes little sense. What we teach and how we teach it are interconnected and addressing them together just makes sense.

Often a single problem can be used to illustrate a number of instructional strategies while exploring specific math content. Consider the following fraction problem:

> Kellen and Liam each took a morning run. Kellen ran $2\frac{1}{4}$ miles. He ran $\frac{3}{4}$ mile more than Liam. How far did Liam run?

As teachers explore and discuss this task, the following content ideas and teaching strategies surface:

- Using number lines as a fraction model to visualize distances
  - Do students associate this situation with a number line model? Why would that model be appropriate to represent this situation? What prior experiences or discussions would help them associate the use of number lines with similar problems?
- Comparison as a subtraction situation—we are comparing the distances Kellen and Liam ran, but in this case we know the difference, but we don't know the distance Liam ran. (Can we use what we know to find the unknown?)
  - Do discussions about the comparison situation in this problem help students make connections to what they already know about whole-number subtraction?
- Using bar models to represent problem situations and see inverse operations—$n + \frac{3}{4} = 2\frac{1}{4}$ or $2\frac{1}{4} - \frac{3}{4} = n$.
  - Does the use of models, and talk about models, help students see the inverse operations?

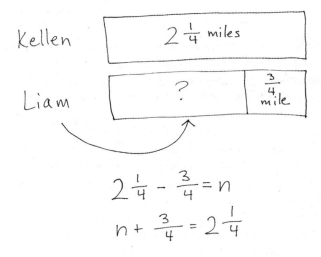

$$2\tfrac{1}{4} - \tfrac{3}{4} = n$$
$$n + \tfrac{3}{4} = 2\tfrac{1}{4}$$

- Building an understanding of the value of fractions—understanding a whole as $\tfrac{4}{4}$ to be able to rename $2\tfrac{1}{4}$ as $1\tfrac{5}{4}$ or simply knowing that $2\tfrac{1}{4} = \tfrac{4}{4} + \tfrac{4}{4} + \tfrac{1}{4}$ which allows us to subtract $\tfrac{3}{4}$.
  - ⊙ Would observing students as they work (formative assessment) provide us with information about whether our students understand these foundational concepts?
- Anticipating what students might do, what might count as evidence of understanding, and what we might do in response.

As teachers explore this problem in professional learning, they are extending their understanding of fractions and exploring instructional strategies like modeling, teacher questioning, making connections to previous learning, and integrating computations and problems. They are expanding their content knowledge and their teaching skills.

Tips for Conducting Highly Effective Workshops

In designing workshops, consider the following key elements to ensure productive sessions.

1. Design activities to keep teachers engaged in the learning. Have at least one hands-on or discussion activity in each segment of the

workshop. Asking teachers to turn and share strategies with partners keeps them engaged and focused on the topic.

2. Respect teachers' knowledge and skills. Praise teachers' efforts, and speak highly of their skills and knowledge. Allow times for participants to share some of their ideas and experience.

3. Do less, but do it well. Introducing too many different activities can be overwhelming to participants. Select just a few activities that illustrate your important points, then weave the activities together by clarifying the big ideas that underlie the activities and why they are productive activities for your students.

4. Reflect on workshop activities, being sure that teachers understand why you presented them in a certain way. After presenting an activity, take a minute to ask teachers to reflect on what they experienced, maybe asking "What were the benefits of this activity?" "What did I do to support your success with the task?" or "What problems could occur with students?"

5. Never forget that you are first and foremost a teacher. Use "we" instead of "you."

6. Be sure that teachers have heard your message. At the end of workshop sessions, have teachers sum up the main points of the session, or take a minute to identify the key ideas from the workshop. Make sure your most important points have been heard.

7. Provide opportunities for session feedback. Assure teachers that their feedback is taken seriously and used to plan future math sessions and meetings. During follow-up sessions, cite feedback and note how it was used to inform the current session.

Both facilitators and participants have common complaints about faculty workshops (see Figures 4.9 and 4.10). How many of the following have you heard? What can we do to minimize these complaints and make our workshops positive experiences for both the facilitators and participants?

Common Teacher Complaints	Scenario	Suggestion
Not engaging	The presenter has a lot of information to share, so decides the quickest way is to tell it, lecturing for forty-five minutes as teachers are beginning to talk among themselves	Be sure to provide a turn-and-share opportunity about every ten minutes to break the "talking to" cycle and engage teachers in the topic. Provide opportunities for teachers to do some activities, even if done in a condensed timeframe.
Can't see the visuals	The presenter scanned a copy of a student worksheet and displayed it on the interactive whiteboard. Teachers are struggling to see the print on the scanned page.	Teachers get quickly frustrated when they cannot read the information on the screen. Provide copies, enlarge the font, or zoom in to allow teachers to see the print.
Can't find activities and ideas in the handouts	The presenter did a quick introductory activity with the participants, and as she continued to present ideas, the teachers began paging through the handouts looking for the activity she just did, distracting them from her additional comments and ideas.	Place the handout page number in the corner of your PowerPoint screen or interactive smartboard page so teachers are reassured that they have the information and so they can easily access it if they want to, allowing them to focus on the session.
Being talked down to or "told" to do something	The presenter tells teachers that "You need to have students talk more in class."	Rather than telling teachers what to do, try less harsh language by suggesting "You might . . . ." Use "we" instead of "you."

Figure 4.9 Common workshop participant complaints

Common Teacher Complaints	Scenario	Suggestion
Lack of respect for their knowledge and skills	The presenter shares lots of ideas and then ends the session without allowing teachers to share any ideas.	Build in opportunities for teachers to share their ideas.
No help to implement the ideas	Following the workshop, teachers are expected to do the strategy in their classrooms but are unsure how.	Offer to provide demonstration lessons or co-teach, if possible. Put the strategy on the agenda for collaborative planning meetings so teachers can discuss how they might implement it. Provide opportunities for teachers to further discuss the ideas, and their implementation of them, at future meetings.
Ideas don't apply to their grade level	The presenter provides a variety of activities at different levels, but teachers notice only the ideas that are at their specific level.	Following an activity, allow teachers to take a couple minutes to talk about how it might be modified for their students. Have teachers discuss the strategies at the next grade-level meeting, focusing on grade-specific applications.

Figure 4.9 Common workshop participant complaints *(cont.)*

Common Facilitator Complaints	Scenario	Suggestion
Teachers are not attentive.	Some teachers are grading papers during the workshop. Others are talking among themselves.	Talk about norms before the session starts. What should teachers be doing during the sessions, and what should they not be doing? Consider how to make the session more engaging!
The teacher focus is on activities, not strategies.	Teachers are talking in the teachers' lounge about the activities presented, but not about the key ideas, or we observe a teacher distributing a worksheet from our workshop but not providing his students with guidance/support the way we demonstrated in our workshop.	Make the strategies explicit by asking teachers to think about and talk about them (e.g., "Just doing this activity is not enough. How would you have to implement it to make it successful?").
There is no follow-up in the classrooms.	Following the workshop on instituting Math Talk charts, we don't see any Math Talk charts in classrooms.	At the end of sessions, set an implementation plan. What will we do this week? What will we do before the next session? Administrator support with this is critical (e.g., "I am excited to see your Math Talk charts during my next walk-through.").
Teachers stop listening when it is near the end of the session.	As soon as the clock strikes 3:00 p.m. (or whenever the workshop is scheduled to end), teachers begin to pack their bags or get up to leave.	End sessions on time. Ending two minutes early will leave everyone feeling positive, while ending two minutes late is often met with frustration and a feeling that we are not respecting teachers' time.

Figure 4.10 Common workshop facilitator complaints

Eliciting and Using Workshop Feedback

Once sessions are done, we want to gather feedback to see what teachers heard and determine next steps. Consider what is most important to know in order to effectively build on the session. You may want to review your current school or district feedback forms to determine if they are really giving you the best information to help you enhance professional learning sessions and determine appropriate next steps.

Some feedback forms ask teachers to evaluate the content knowledge of the presenter. Would a novice or mathphobic teacher be the best person to assess the presenter's knowledge? Might that be better evaluated by the math coach, district math specialist, or school leader? Does your feedback form ask for teachers to assign number scores to feedback criteria, rating the session on a 1–7 scale in which some teachers say "Absolutely the best session I have ever attended!" and rate it a 5 or 6? How do those ratings help you in your future planning? What do you really want to know in order to assess the effectiveness of the session?

- *What did the teachers learn from this? What insights did they gain?*
- *What do they have questions about or find confusing?*
- *In what areas do they need further help?*
- *What are they planning to try in their classrooms, and in what ways might they need help for implementation?*
- *What would they like to see as next steps?*

These types of questions allow you to gather information to assist teachers in their learning and to plan further professional learning opportunities for them. The questions might be a part of feedback forms as in Figure 4.11 or simply questions for teachers to answer on the two sides of an index card like the following:

Side 1: What did you expect from this session?

Side 2: What did you get from this session?

Side 1: An insight that changes my math teaching

Side 2: A question I still have

Side 1: What I got from this session

Side 2: What I still need

Feedback

Please complete the following statements to provide feedback on today's session.

What I hoped to learn…	What I learned…
What I am going to try…	I'd like to know more about…

Share Your Ideas

Please share your ideas below to provide feedback on today's session.

An instructional technique that I feel would improve my students' math skills is…
An activity I am going to try is…
An insight I had…
I am still wondering about…

A full-size template for these are available in the online resources.

Figure 4.11 Feedback forms

MORE IDEAS FOR PROFESSIONAL LEARNING

Teaching can be quite isolating. Teachers are in their own classrooms with their students throughout the day. During walk-throughs, we are able to see the different styles and strategies used by various teachers, but they rarely get that same opportunity to see others teach. Consider options to provide teachers with insights about teaching by helping them look outside their own classrooms.

Peer Observation

Through peer observations, teachers work with colleagues to observe each other's math teaching strategies and to observe students' learning. Peer observations can be a way for the visiting teacher to gather new strategies, or it can be a way for the observed teacher to gather peer feedback to enhance her teaching.

Peer observations can be initiated either by the observer or by the teacher being observed. A teacher might request to visit a particular colleague to see a problem-solving lesson after seeing his students' expertise with math problems. A teacher might request a colleague to observe her to see how well she is doing at asking deep questions. Or the school leader or math coach might initiate peer observations for certain teachers who would benefit from seeing particular strategies.

Any observations are more valuable when they are focused. In order to ensure that the visits are productive, the observing and visiting teachers might be asked to talk briefly prior to the visit to set goals for the observations. What types of strategies would the visiting teacher like to observe? Or what is the teacher working on about which he would like the visitor's feedback? The visiting teacher is asked to share simple but directed feedback following the observation. A simple technique is Praise—Question—Polish (see Figure 4.12) in which the visitor jots down (1) a positive comment about what she saw during the lesson, (2) a question she might ask the teacher about why she chose a particular task, strategy, or grouping format, and (3) an idea or suggestion that might enhance the lesson or simply offer a different approach.

These visits can be set up during times when the visiting teacher's students are at lunch, recess, or specials, or, when possible, the visiting teacher might be given an opportunity to observe while her class is taught by a school specialist or substitute teacher. Schools that have university interns (student teachers) sometimes schedule peer observations for their mentor teachers during the interns' full takeover time when the teachers are able to leave the classrooms for short periods.

Praise—I liked this!

Question—Why did you . . . ?

Polish—An idea I had . . .

Figure 4.12 Teacher-to-teacher feedback

Exploring Teaching Through Video-Recorded Lessons

While it can be a great opportunity to observe teaching in other classrooms in real time, the logistics of arranging these visits can be problematic. Another option for observing real teaching is through videotaped lessons. Video clips allow us to view snippets of a lesson rather than watching a lesson from start to finish, and they allow us to pause the action in order to discuss our observations and insights. Consider the following options.

VIDEO RECORDING TEACHERS WITHIN YOUR DISTRICT OR SCHOOL

It can be powerful to compile your own library of videotaped math lessons that show teaching with your curriculum and students. Many districts have created these videos for use by school leaders and math coaches, asking some of their expert math teachers to demonstrate specific strategies or show specific content lessons. This can be a great way to personalize the videos to the strategies being focused on by the school or district. One drawback may be the familiarity with the teachers who have been videotaped. When observing math lessons, an important discussion point is "What might the teacher have done differently?" This question can be awkward when the teachers are known by those observing the video clips.

VIDEO RECORDING AS A COACHING STRATEGY

We have mentioned the importance of teachers transferring the information they gather in professional development workshops or group meetings into their actual teaching in the classroom. However, this can be a difficult transition. Seeing video of their own teaching helps teachers assess their skills with the newly acquired strategies and pinpoint ways to improve their delivery of lessons. In addition, videos show not just the teacher but the students, allowing teachers to observe and notice what students are doing as they are teaching math. Who is engaged? Who is distracted? Who appears to be having difficulty?

Offering to video record teachers as a reflective strategy is a great coaching option. Once a lesson is recorded, teachers simply take the video home and observe themselves at their leisure and in private. They then return to school ready to discuss their insights with the math coach, the school leader, or their colleagues.

USING VIDEO CLIPS AS A PROFESSIONAL LEARNING ACTIVITY

Incorporating video of math teaching enhances professional learning sessions. It bridges the transition from talking about how to do it to doing it on your own. When teachers actually see the strategies being implemented with students, they begin to envision the ideas and consider how to apply them in their own math classrooms.

Watching a video of math teaching opens up the possibility for extensive conversation around a number of topics. Teachers might talk about the math content, the questions the teacher asked, the materials she used, and the interactions she had with students. They might comment on students' knowledge and skills and how they identified them (formative assessment) and likely even notice seating arrangements, Math Talk charts, and bulletin boards within the videotaped classroom.

When using video to promote teacher discussion and reflection, it is best to use brief clips rather than viewing an entire lesson. In that way, the majority of time is spent on discussion and reflection. Focusing teachers' attention with some guiding questions or "look fors" can be helpful. For a video clip focusing on promoting math talk, the facilitator might ask teachers to think about the following:

1. What did the teacher ask students to talk about? Give some specific examples.
2. What did you observe about the students' verbalizations? Give some specific examples.
3. How did the teacher respond to students' verbalizations? Give some specific examples.
4. How can a teacher create a classroom environment in which students feel comfortable taking the risk of expressing their ideas, right or wrong?

Or teachers might be given recording sheets to jot down their observations, along with their thoughts, questions, and insights as they view the video (see Figure 4.13). These notes allow teachers to think back to the video during the post-video discussions. Using brief video clips allows you to show the video again, after some discussion, to revisit the teachers' strategies.

The best videos are those that are not overly edited but show actual teaching as it happens. Teaching is about making decisions, and there are usually multiple ways to respond to students or classroom situations, so seeing the way a teacher responded and then conjecturing about other possibilities promotes reflection about the decisions we make and the actions we take.

Strategy being observed:	
Observations	Comments? Insights? Questions?

This form is available in the online resources.

Figure 4.13 Observing teaching from a video clip

The Math in Practice series offers a video library with clips of teachers working in *real* classrooms with *real* students. The clips focus on the critical teaching strategies highlighted throughout the series.

Opportunities to Share Ideas

QUICK GLIMPSE OF STANDARDS ACROSS THE YEARS

Take a few minutes at a faculty meeting to highlight math standards progressions with a quick share across grade levels. Designate a particular math topic (e.g., place value, problem solving, math facts, geometric shapes). Have each grade level share the big ideas about that topic that are focused on at that level, so teachers become familiar with the progression of skills K–5.

QUICK LINKS

Mark a date on your calendar, maybe once or twice a month, to send a quick email with a couple of links related to your math professional development topics. The math coach or district math supervisor can help you identify fun and valuable online resources. Keep the list short and useful.

LENDING LIBRARY

Establish a lending library with math teacher resource books. Take a few minutes at the start of faculty meetings or grade-level meetings to introduce a book and share an idea from that book to generate interest.

TIPS FOR TEACHERS FROM TEACHERS

Consider compiling your own "tips" collection by asking teachers to share a tip about a specific topic (e.g., teaching basic facts, modeling fractions, building problem-solving skills). Share a few at faculty meetings or send an email with the list of tips.

MATH IDEA SWAP

Invite teachers to an informal math swap one afternoon each month, and decide on a topic. Teachers can drop in to share an idea or gather ideas from their peers. Always have a few ideas to share with the group, so you know that they will always leave with some new ideas.

Planning for Professional Learning

While our focus in this chapter is on the goals, topics, and execution of professional learning, we can't forget the logistical issues that surface when planning these opportunities for our teachers. While as a profession we acknowledge the importance of professional learning, we have not allocated sufficient time and resources to make it happen for our teachers. Unlike most professions, teachers are with their students for the majority of their work hours. Time allocated for professional learning is usually brief. And money to fund professional learning is often insufficient. Where do we find the time and money to provide these critical experiences?

FINDING TIME FOR PROFESSIONAL LEARNING

It is a sad reality that most districts have dramatically cut professional development days from their school calendars. The few days before the start of the school year are rarely enough time for teachers to set up their classrooms, prepare class materials, review curriculum documents, and prepare for the start of the year. And the few days at the end of the school year are filled with such tasks as teachers cleaning their classrooms, organizing and storing supplies, recording notes for the following year's teachers, or the variety of other custodial tasks that need to be done to wrap up the year. Some of the days during the year on which students do not report to school are designated as parent conference days or grading days and are not able to be used for professional learning. Finding time for professional learning requires commitment and creativity.

Our first step is to determine how to best use the professional learning days that are built into our school calendars. If they are at the start of the year, do we kick off schoolwide or grade-level initiatives during the meetings, maybe discussing student achievement data, developing buy-in from teachers, and discussing some relevant research-driven instructional strategies? Do we use the sessions to effectively begin a year-long effort related to a meaningful math topic? Do we identify just the right facilitator to energize the staff and set the tone for the coming year?

During the school year, do we capitalize on the available designated professional learning days by scheduling sessions to maintain our momentum and continue the learning? Do we make sure the sessions are meaningful and filled with practical strategies so teachers remain engaged and committed to our plan? Do we provide opportunities for teachers to reflect on their progress, as well as opportunities to frequently review student work related to our goals?

If our professional learning days are at the end of the year, do we use them to reflect on progress throughout the year and to identify successes and discuss continued needs? Do we set goals for the following year? Do we introduce new strategies and ideas that can be pondered over the summer months or suggest books for summer learning?

With limited days in most district calendars for professional learning, we have to rethink our "all or nothing" philosophy, recognizing that finding a whole day may be quite difficult, but finding short periods of time spread throughout the year may be doable and better supports our understanding of the value of ongoing learning. Can we capitalize on half-days or even hour-long chunks of time to weave together significant professional learning? Consider the following:

- Could we use grade-level meeting times to provide short, focused learning opportunities?
- Could we designate days throughout the year in which we provide substitute teachers who may rotate from grade level to grade level throughout the day, allowing teachers to meet for one- or two-hour sessions?
- Can our school schedule be designed so that grade-levels share music, physical education, art, or other special classes in order to allow grade-level teachers time to meet, plan, and reflect on student learning on a regular basis?
- How do we use the time before and after students arrive in the buildings? Can teams meet before students arrive in the buildings or after they are dismissed?
- How do we use our faculty meeting times? Can some topics addressed at faculty meetings be handled through emails to allow more time for discussions about teaching and learning? Can five or ten minutes of each faculty meeting be designated for teachers to share a math strategy or success?
- Are Saturday or Summer Mathematics Teacher Academies possible? Teachers attend professional learning if it engages them and meets their needs. Alternative funding including Title I, Title II, district funds, or grants may be an option for schools to provide Saturday or Summer Academies.

The solution to finding time for professional learning will be different for each school or district. Some districts have shown their commitment to teachers by extending the school day by five or ten minutes each day and using the extra time to designate early dismissals once each month to allow an afternoon of professional learning for teachers. In other buildings teachers are able to leave shortly after student dismissal most days, pooling that time for a lengthier after-school session once or twice each month.

Not all of these solutions will be doable for, or acceptable to, all school leaders, but what can you live with? It is understandable that many districts do not want substitute teachers to be in classrooms while teachers engage in professional learning. It is, of course, preferred to have a highly-skilled math teacher with students as much as possible, but if our teachers need support to understand what they are teaching, or to identify and refine effective strategies to promote student learning, is it better to have a substitute with students for a few hours or to continue to allow a teacher to teach without support? Would that half-day outside the classroom, focused on building teachers' efficacy, make a long-term difference for all students?

Funding Professional Learning

As district and school leaders, it is important that we defend the need for professional learning for our teachers, including lobbying for both time and funds to support professional learning experiences. We must also advocate for math coaches in our schools. Clearly, this position is costly, but the benefits are invaluable. This specialist not only consults with the school leader on math issues and guides math program decisions but also provides day-to-day support to teachers by facilitating planning meetings, conducting workshops, leading study groups, providing co-teaching and demonstrations in classrooms, and offering a wealth of whole-staff and one-to-one professional learning options.

Funding for professional learning should be a part of a district or school budget, but finding alternate funding sources is often necessary. Through federal programs, grants, PTA budget contributions, and other creative funding sources, schools and districts are able to augment their budgets for ongoing learning opportunities for their teachers. We too often set aside professional learning for teachers because we must spend money on expensive textbooks and other materials, and yet investment in developing high-quality math teachers is one of the soundest decisions we can make. A highly skilled math teacher knows math content, understands standards, and has a repertoire of strategies that make a difference in our children's learning. Imagine how fortunate a district would be to have this type of teacher in each elementary math classroom—a return well worth the investment!

Questions for Reflection

- How do we identify professional development needs in our building?

- How can we make professional learning ongoing in our building?

- What next steps do we initiate as a result of professional learning experiences?

- What professional learning sessions have been successful for our teachers? Why have they been successful? How did they help our teachers?

- How do we engage teachers during professional learning sessions?

- How do we look for the impact of faculty study groups? Do teachers share their learning with others who weren't in the group? Do they apply the learning in their classrooms?

- What successes or challenges have we had with book studies in our building?

- What opportunities do our teachers have to watch colleagues or themselves teach?

- How do we find the time and funding for professional learning?

Parents as Partners

Working collaboratively with parents ensures that our students hear positive messages about math and get math support whether at home or at school. By welcoming parents into our schools, listening to their concerns, sharing our teaching practices, communicating about their child's progress, and coordinating programs to acquaint them with current math standards and teaching, we forge a partnership that benefits all parties.

What Parents Need to Hear from Us

As we have discussed, the mathematics classroom we encourage today is quite different from those that we and our students' parents remember. These contrasting approaches to mathematics teaching and learning understandably raise questions from parents and the community. Parents simply want their children to be successful. They trust us to make that happen and get nervous when math homework or classwork appears different from what they remember. So it's not surprising that many parents request that familiar approach to mathematics instruction for their own children, even as they may quip that they were never any good in mathematics and did not enjoy or find their math classes valuable.

Like the rest of us, parents may hold unproductive beliefs about mathematics that have grown out of their own experience: that you're either good at math or you aren't, that there is only one way to do math, that math is all about right answers and speed, that using calculators and other tools is "cheating."

It is important to remember that we as educators have had opportunities to explore and digest the changes in math teaching, but many parents have not had the opportunity to hear about what has changed and why it has changed, leaving them feeling confused and frustrated. Parents may have heard sensationalized stories about math instruction. Many are unable to visit math classrooms during the day. They learn about mathematics instruction from what their children share, the class-work or homework they see, or conversations they have with other parents at the soccer field. This leads to all sorts of questions and misunderstandings. It is up to us and the teachers we work with to communicate these changes, what they mean, and why they matter.

Parents should hear from us that

1. **These changes are about helping their children.** We want their children to understand and be able to use math. We want to avoid creating the anxiety about mathematics that many adults today have.
2. **These changes make sense and occurred over time as we learned more about the teaching and learning of mathematics.** In the past, some students were able to get it on their own, but many were not. Today, we want *all* students to learn mathematics, and we believe they all can.
3. **Parents play an important role in the change.** When parents remain positive about the math being taught, students are more positive about the strategies they are being taught. Parents can help by talking positively about math and being open to new strategies and activities.

We also need to reassure parents that their children are learning "real math," and that

1. Math content has not changed. $\frac{1}{2}$ and $\frac{2}{4}$ are still equivalent fractions. $20 + 30$ still equals 50. The difference today is that students are taught to understand math skills and concepts before memorizing procedures.
2. Computations, including the standard algorithms parents probably remember, are still taught, but understanding and application are also taught. And

algorithms are introduced after students have learned number-based ways to find answers and can understand why the algorithms work. We want students to have a range of flexible strategies to use, choosing appropriate ones for different situations.

3. Problem solving is not an afterthought or an enrichment activity at the bottom of the textbook page. Instead, it is part of everything we teach.
4. There is not just one way to get an answer. We have choices as to how we find answers, but all of them require an understanding of math.

And parents should most definitely hear the following about what we expect from their children:

1. All students can do and enjoy math.
2. We are more confident with something when we understand what we are doing.
3. Mistakes are part of the process. Rather than being punished for them, we use them to investigate and discuss the math ideas and learn from them.
4. We expect all students to try and to persevere.
5. We expect students to talk about the math they do so we can figure out what they understand and what they don't, and so we can find ways to help them.

At the end of this chapter, we have included a list of questions parents frequently ask, with some suggestions to help you respond.

How We Can Help: Fostering Parent Relationships

Building partnership with parents begins with listening to parents and welcoming them into our schools and classrooms. It is built upon communication that is timely and consistent and is enhanced when we provide opportunities to build relationships through schoolwide math events and specific parent-involvement activities.

LISTENING TO PARENTS

We want our schools to be positive, welcoming places. The same should be true about our mathematics program. It is important that we listen to parents and work to understand their concerns. We must also be understanding of their ideas about teaching and learning mathematics. After all, it is likely that we once fostered some of those same ideas.

As administrators, we know the importance of listening to concerns of staff and community. It is critical that we demonstrate this for mathematics instruction as well. First and foremost, we establish open-door policies and make sure we are accessible to parents who want to talk about math instruction, being willing to meet with those who have concerns or suggestions. We might develop parent mathematics advisory committees or even start yearly feedback forums. And we pass this open-door philosophy on to the teachers in our buildings. We want our teachers to feel trusted and supported, but we also want to develop their commitment to listening to parent concerns.

COMMUNICATING WITH PARENTS

As discussed in the previous section, we want to make sure parents know what is going on in our classrooms and why. Following are some ways we can share information with parents about their children and about mathematics in our schools.

Digital Tools and Newsletters

Communication about our math program is essential. In the past, written newsletters were often sent home, sharing brief reports of classroom and school programs, but with a digital, web-based format, schools are able to share program information online, allowing for immediate updates, as well as the inclusion of photos and videos of program events. Featured events and activities can be strategically selected to demonstrate our focus on solving problems, modeling math ideas, using varied tools, or performing collaborative work. A monthly feature might be to focus on a math topic or standard, explaining its importance as well as providing examples of how it might look in math classrooms (e.g., the importance of modeling math ideas, justifying answers, understanding computational procedures, or building students' number sense).

Linking classrooms to the school website allows parents to access up-to-date information on math activities within their children's classrooms. Classroom math investigations can be featured, or student work can be highlighted. Teachers might post the math standards they are currently exploring in class and even post short videos to show the strategies that students are learning. Tips for helping with home-work might be included, and links to math games and resources that support the skills students are learning can be shared. Our websites should help spread the word about our math priorities and celebrate the success of our students and teachers.

Parent Conferences

Parent conferences are our chance to have a dialogue with parents about their child's progress and success, as well as an opportunity to discuss concerns. It can also be an opportunity to inadvertently convey the wrong messages. Before con-ferences, it is wise for us to revisit expectations with staff, reinforcing our confi-dence and pride in them as professionals. We remind staff that parents are likely to remember bad mathematics experiences or may have math anxiety themselves. Relying on conveying objective data and sharing examples of student work help us stay focused on what the student can do and ways to help him. Identifying resources, strategies, and/or activities to share with parents to support their child's mathematics progress reminds parents that we want the best for their child.

Schoolwide Math Events

Schoolwide mathematics events are prime opportunities to showcase our program, our students, and our teaching. They should be positive, engaging, and celebrate the joy of learning math! We capitalize on the opportunity to highlight student work and achievement during these events either verbally or by displaying them in public spaces in the building. Some types of events that have proven successful follow.

Back-to-School Night

Back-to-School Night is generally the most highly attended parent event as they come to school to learn about the coming year and meet their child's new teacher. As teachers meet parents and present an overview of the coming year, they provide some insights into what will be taught in mathematics, as well as how it will be taught, paving the way for better understanding as the year progresses. Teachers might display math manipulatives or resource books so parents have an oppor-tunity to see instructional materials. Parents might be given a list of skills and standards (in parent-friendly language) so they know what their children will be learning throughout the year. This is a great opportunity for teachers to reinforce the importance of thinking and problem solving as well as reassuring parents that basic skills are still important.

Family Math Nights

See the online resources for a sample Family Math Night letter, agenda, and parent feedback form.

Family Math Nights are programs in which parents and children share an evening of math activities. Parent and child might move through stations in a series of self-directed explorations, or they might participate in teacher- or volunteer-directed activities in which they explore a variety of mathematical ideas. The evenings offer hands-on activities like basic math fact games and strategies, data collection and analysis tasks, exploration of geometry concepts through tangram or pattern-block activities or card games to explore fraction or decimal concepts. In most cases, the games are sent home for continued parent/child play. Family Math Nights promote parent/child involvement, create an awareness of math strategies and standards, stimulate excitement for mathematics, and nurture positive attitudes about mathematics. For activity ideas, try the *Family Math* series from EQUALS, Lawrence Hall of Science, University of California at Berkeley (http://equals.lhs.berkeley.edu).

Math Fairs

For a list of possible Math Fair projects, see the online resources.

Math Fairs are a way for students to display math projects and for parents to see the diverse ways in which math touches students' lives. Students choose projects that connect to their math interests and may work alone or with a partner. Projects are displayed at an evening gathering where families are able to view many children's projects as they take special pride in the work of their own child. Student projects might include designing math board games, designing and conducting a survey and graphing the results, creating a tessellation, designing a logic matrix problem, or designing a series of number or shape patterns. Math Fairs allow students to choose a math activity that matches their interests and highlights the varied applications of mathematics.

Math Carnivals

Math Carnivals are active events in which children engage in math at various booths, such as a long jump in which students must measure the length of their jumps, or spinner games in which students receive points based on their spins. Students might score points for tossing bean bags into different-colored circles marked on the playground blacktop or pluck plastic ducks from a pond with math facts written underneath in which the answers determine their score. Traditional carnival games of tossing rings or guessing height are all adapted to the math theme. Math Fairs are fun and active and focus on math skills from measurement to money to geometry to basic facts.

INTERACTIVE OPEN HOUSE EVENTS

If your school has an open house in which parents visit during the school day, encourage teachers to plan an interactive activity in which parents are invited to sit alongside their children and participate in the activity. Rather than the traditional experience of standing along the fringes of the classroom and watching their children do math, parents are engaged in playing games to review basic facts or using geoboards to explore symmetry or creating posters to show math concepts. The activities are fun and interactive and give them insight into ways they might work with their children at home (see Figure 5.1).

Promoting Math at Home

Another way to communicate our math goals to parents is by encouraging them to incorporate math activities and math talk into their lives at home, just as we encourage them to read with their children. Encourage your teachers to suggest some of these ideas.

FAMILY MATH GAME NIGHT

Suggest a Family Game Night and provide parents with ideas of common games that reinforce math skills. Younger students might practice comparing whole numbers as they play the card game War, extend their understanding of spatial relationships at they build with blocks, develop their logical reasoning skills by playing checkers, or practice their counting skills as they move spaces in Candyland. Older students might apply their money skills to play Monopoly, use their understanding of coordinate grids to play Battleship, or apply their logical reasoning skills to play chess, Connect Four, or Mastermind. Reminding parents of the important math skills that can be reinforced by playing common card or board games helps them see that they can build their children's math skills and have fun while doing it.

Figure 5.1 Giving parents opportunities to see their children doing math helps them understand our techniques and priorities.

See the children's literature list in the Math in Practice: A Guide for Teachers online resources.

MATH READING

Send home a list of children's books that support the math ideas that they are exploring in class. Encourage parents to read with their children at home and then discuss the math from the story. Invite parents to come to math class on a special day to read a favorite math-related book to the class.

Math Month Calendar

April is Math Month. It is a perfect opportunity to send home a calendar of fun, daily math activities that families can do together. This gives parents a glimpse into at-home activities that promote positive attitudes about math and reinforce math skills.

Math Backpacks

Develop some take-home kits or backpacks for students to check out for parent/ child home use. (Encourage grade-level or grade-band teachers to work together to develop these kits for students.) Each kit should contain materials and directions for a parent/child hands-on activity: a small clock with movable hands and some cards with various times for students to show on the clock, or a ruler and a list of items to estimate and then measure, or a tangram and some pictures of tangrams arranged in animal shapes for parent and child to replicate.

Math Interviews

Involve students in talking to their parents about the math their parents use each day at home and at work. Students might interview parents and report to the class on the ways in which their parents use math. Inviting students to share what they learn allows the whole class to hear the many ways that math is used across all walks of life.

Summer Math Fun

Provide parents with a list of fun summer activities that reinforce math skills and concepts. It might include ideas for board games that use math skills, ideas for visits to nearby museums or learning centers, books to check out at the library that have a math message, or activities to do while driving or grocery shopping.

It is our responsibility to help parents understand the changes we are implementing in math classrooms. We can allay their fears and help them embrace these changes when we open our schools and classrooms to them, listen to their concerns and answer their questions, and provide ongoing opportunities for them to see and better understand our math programs. At all times, our goal is to help parents see that their children are our priority and that we are striving to help them understand and love math (see Figure 5.2). With the support of parents, our efforts to change attitudes and achievement in mathematics can be significant and lasting.

> See the online resources for K–5 math month calendars that can be used as is or modified to include your favorite activities.

Figure 5.2 Our priority is giving students the best math experience possible.

Frequently Asked Questions

The following are some questions parents frequently ask about mathematics instruction, with some ideas for how you and your teachers can answer them. This list is just a beginning; you know your own community best and will be able to adapt these answers or create new ones to meet your needs. You might consider spending a faculty meeting, or professional development time, with your teaching teams brainstorming other questions they have encountered, answers to those questions, and ways to share those answers effectively with parents.

In some cases, we have provided sample answers; in others, we suggest ways to address the question with parents more generally through communication and activities.

QUESTIONS ABOUT THE MATH PROGRAM

What are your goals for the elementary mathematics program?

We want all students to have conceptual understanding (knowing important mathematical ideas), procedural fluency (the ability to calculate and use other mathematical skills effectively), problem-solving and application skills (the ability to use math to deal with real-world situations), and a positive attitude about math. We want *all* students, not just a few "math people," to be able to think and reason mathematically, solve problems, communicate their ideas, model their thinking, and make connections between math concepts. We have high expectations for all students and believe that all students can learn mathematics.

What do the standards (or objectives) mean?

It is important to outline for parents what their student will learn during the year. However, printing standards and sending them home at Back-to-School Night might not be the best idea. The language of our standards documents can be vague, misleading, and confusing without training and experience (and even with it!). Instead, it is wise to put standards into parent-friendly terms and provide illustrations or examples as needed. When doing so, we have to be careful to avoid misrepresenting the intent of the standard.

These ideas can be shared in different ways. Grade-level teams, or grade bands, can create short brochures to communicate mathematics content or include this information in periodic math newsletters. Some schools dedicate part of their website to mathematics instruction and include links to high-quality resources. Family Math Nights, Math Open Houses, and Back-to-School Nights are also opportunities for communicating the mathematics that students are learning.

Why does the mathematics look different than when I was in elementary school?

We want our students to understand mathematics as well as do mathematics. To achieve this, we use many different representations (e.g., hands-on materials, number lines, and diagrams) and strategies for making sense of numbers, operations, and problems. While the traditional approaches worked for some students, many other students did not succeed, leaving them with poorly memorized procedures that they did not know how to apply, confusion about key math ideas, and often a very negative view of math. We want to change these outcomes, so we have needed to change our instruction.

QUESTIONS ABOUT CHANGES IN MATH INSTRUCTION

What are the different tools and pictures our students are using?

Many adults have had limited experiences with the representations and tools used for modeling mathematics in elementary school. Some tools, such as base-ten blocks and number lines, are straightforward and clearly connected to math concepts. Others, such as ten frames, pattern blocks, and bar diagrams, may feel foreign to parents.

Many schools and teachers have had success compiling notes and diagrams to explain how the tool or representation supports the mathematics. Others have embedded the tools in Back-to-School Nights and Family Math Nights in order to familiarize parents with them. Still others have communicated ideas about the tools through school newsletters, websites, and math brochures for parents. Regardless of the method, the important takeaway is for teachers, teams, and schools to communicate mathematics tools and representations with parents. Just as students need to be introduced to each new representation, so too do their parents. It's helpful to include what the tool or representation is, how it works, and how students use it so that parents are engaged and empowered to help their students at home.

It is not uncommon for parents to ask why students have to work with all of these representations when traditional algorithms are straightforward and easy to complete. In cases like this, we need to help parents understand that

- the algorithm appears straightforward to adults who have been using it for years, but it is often meaningless to students, leading to errors because they do not understand what they are doing
- students are more successful when understanding the math before doing it procedurally. Working with these representations builds understanding and improves the likelihood of success with the algorithm in the future.

Why do students need to have more than one strategy? Can't they just do it the same way?

Having many different strategies, and knowing when to use them, allows students to choose the strategy that works best for a specific situation. Consider 99 + 3. We could solve it with the algorithm on paper. But that is not very efficient. Instead, we could count on 3 more from 99, or give 1 from 3 to 99 to make 100 and change the problem to 100 + 2, either of which is probably faster for us to do mentally than using paper and pencil. But we might use a different strategy to solve 99 + 72 or 173 + 75.

Many adults already do this kind of mental math in their daily lives! But they may think that it doesn't count as "real math," because they were taught that they had to use one particular method or algorithm. It is important to reassure parents that this is very much real math, and it demonstrates a flexible understanding of numbers that they may not realize that they have. This explanation can help them see why we want their children to have similar flexibility.

It is important for parents to understand that, while we want all students to be exposed to and try a variety of strategies, the goal is not for all students to use the same strategy to solve the same problem. Rather, students are prompted to use strategies that make sense to them depending on the numbers, context, and/or situation of the problem.

Why do students need to explain their thinking? Isn't it enough to get the right answer?

Today, mathematics is more than just getting correct answers. Being able to communicate our ideas and justify our thinking is an important skill, and not just in mathematics. By requiring students to share and justify their ideas, we help them clarify their thinking and learn to communicate it well. We can also learn about potential misconceptions or conceptual misunderstandings to gain insight into where they may be coming from, so we can find ways to help.

Why don't we just use formulas?

We do want our students to learn formulas, such as those for finding area in geometry. However, we want them to remember the formulas long after the class period, unit, or year has ended. To do this, we establish the meaning behind the formulas before introducing and practicing them.

Why don't they just practice the basics? Shouldn't I be seeing lots of worksheets with practice problems?

We absolutely want our students to be able to understand, retain, and apply key "basic" skills such as knowing basic facts and being able to use computation procedures. But we now know that students are more successful with computations and algorithms if they understand the concepts that underlie them. We transition to practicing skills and procedures after students show understanding of underlying concepts. Even then, practice is purposeful, focusing on reinforcing concepts, procedures, and problem-solving activities. It can include practice sheets or hands-on activities, but a noticeable difference with mathematics practice today is the number of isolated computation problems students are assigned. We have realized that when students are given lengthy worksheets, several things may happen.

1. The length of the task creates immediate anxiety for many students, frustrating them and causing them to shut down.
2. They tend to speed through the worksheet in an effort to get done quickly. This often results in careless errors and little attention to what they are doing.
3. Students who make errors often make the same error over and over, ultimately memorizing the wrong way of doing the computation, making it more challenging for us to reteach the skill.

When we adjust the length of the task, we often find that shorter sets of practice allow us to identify and fix errors more efficiently, do not overwhelm students, and result in fewer errors and more attention to the actual math task. They may not be doing as many repetitions, but they are focusing more on the ones they are doing.

What about the basic facts? Don't kids still need to memorize their times tables? What about timed tests?

Over the years, we have learned that "basic facts" may be one of the biggest mis-
nomers in education. We've tried flashcards and timed tests for decades, and still
too many kids don't end up knowing the facts as well as we'd like. We have learned
that students learn better when they understand what operations mean and the
relationships between them and how numbers can be broken apart. With these
understandings, they don't have to rely just on rote memory but can use those relationships to quickly figure out any facts they might otherwise lose track of.

But make no mistake: The goal of basic fact instruction continues to be that our
students are able to recall facts. Today, we develop basic fact fluency by focusing on
understanding and targeted instruction. We teach related facts together and follow
instruction with practice, independent activities, and games that build fluency.
Sharing these activities and games with parents to use at home can enable them not
only to help their children learn but to understand what we are doing in our math
instruction and why.

Timed tests and flash-card drills, while effective for some students, do not
produce good results for all students and, in fact, cause exactly the anxiety and
damaged attitudes about math that we want to avoid. While we want to know that
students have learned their facts, we can use other assessments to monitor their
progress without relying on traditional speed drills.

Why aren't you covering everything? Where are the important concepts like time and money?

We do still teach time, money, measurement, and other concepts, because they are
important—but these are not the *most* important concepts for our students to learn.
Ideas such as multidigit computation, problem solving, and fractions are consid-
erably more important math concepts because they provide foundational understandings and skills that are needed for success in middle and high school math.
We spend more time on these number concepts because other math relies on our
students' understanding of them. In fact, these number concepts form the basis for
understanding money, measurement, time, and other math skills.

Sharing with parents the key ideas from each grade band can help them understand how we allot the time we spend on math instruction. In K–2, we focus on
counting and number decomposition, place value and comparisons, and addition

and subtraction. In grades 3–5, we focus on place value with larger numbers, multiplication and division, and fraction concepts. And at all grade levels, we focus on problem solving.

Encourage parents to work with their students at home on concepts of time, money, and measurement. These concepts are important parts of daily life and thus are easy to work into ordinary conversations. They can also provide useful contexts for discussions of number and operations.

QUESTIONS ABOUT HELPING AT HOME

My child is struggling with all these different strategies. Why shouldn't I just show him the way I learned to do it? It's quicker!

It is important for us to communicate to parents the different strategies and approaches used at school. It is also important that we refrain from insisting that students use particular approaches, methods, or procedures for working with concepts. However, when this question arises, it is usually in reference to parents showing their child a standard algorithm for multidigit addition, subtraction, multiplication, or division. Conversations with parents about the introduction of standard algorithms are critical. The focus of these discussions is on timing—asking parents to give us the time to develop these computational procedures through strategies and models that are based on an understanding of numbers and place value. Once their child understands the process, we introduce the standard algorithms. Allowing teachers time to build understanding ultimately helps children develop a stronger number sense and a deeper understanding of what they are doing. Assure parents that the algorithm will be taught, and that we are in no rush to teach it right away, but would rather slow down the process so students understand what they are doing. Once the standard algorithm is introduced, they can jump in and share their approach.

How can I help my child with her homework if I don't understand it?

Practicing mathematics at home is important for student success. Parents should be encouraged to work with their students in many ways, including going over homework, having math conversations in the real world (restaurants, stores, sporting events), and playing games. Parents may struggle, though, if they feel that they don't understand the homework themselves.

The parent communication ideas we discussed earlier are critical here. Websites, newsletters, conferences, and math nights are all ways to help parents understand the math their children are doing. (Finding or developing these resources can be a good project for a school mathematics team as described in Chapter 1.) Encourage teachers to include example problems with the homework assignments so that parents have something to refer to. And asking teachers to consistently assure parents that when their child is unable to complete the task, and they are unable to assist them, alerting the teacher is the reasonable next step, so we can take it from there and revisit the skill in class.

Parents can help in more ways than just working on homework: Playing math games, asking questions about math skills and concepts while going about daily routines such as driving or shopping, and performing other activities such as counting buttons, having scavenger hunts around the house for examples of fractions, or looking for examples of acute angles are also great ways to practice mathematics at home.

Parents will have a myriad of questions about math standards, skills, and teaching strategies. Rather than being frustrated by their many questions, we should consider the opportunity their questions bring. The articulation of these questions allows their fears and concerns to surface, giving us the chance to address them and begin to shift attitudes and clarify misunderstandings about our math programs.

Resources for Parent Programs

Boaler, Jo. 2015. *What's Math Got to Do with It?* New York: Penguin Books.

Coates, Grace Davila, and Jean Kerr Stenmark. 1997. *Family Math for Young Children.* Berkeley, CA: Regents of the University of California.

Coates, Grace Davila, and Virginia Thompson. 2003. *Family Math II: Achieving Success in Mathematics.* Berkeley, CA: Regents of the University of California.

Danielson, Christopher. 2015. *Common Core Math for Parents for Dummies.* Hoboken, NJ: John Wiley & Sons.

Stenmark, Jean Kerr, Virginia Thompson, and Ruth Cossey. 1986. *Family Math*. Berkeley, CA: Regents of the University of California.

Whitenack, Joy, Laurie O. Cavey, and Catherine Henney. 2015. *It's Elementary: A Parent's Guide to K-5 Mathematics*. Reston, VA: National Council of Teachers of Mathematics.

Questions for Reflection

- How do we frame mathematics conferences? When do we offer them? How do we evaluate their impact on our school community?

- What math events do we host that engage parents and promote our program?

- What are the math topics that parents inquire about most frequently in our school?

Conclusion

Our vision of elementary mathematics has changed, and our programs and teaching are challenged to change along with it. The changes are focused on making math more accessible, understandable, and meaningful for our students. These changes are about providing a strong foundation to transition our students smoothly into the more complex skills and concepts addressed in the middle grades. They are also about generating enthusiasm, inquiry, and, yes, even love of mathematics!

These changes have been suggested for the last couple of decades, supported by our leading math organizations like the National Council of Teachers of Mathematics, and grounded in research. But making these changes challenges our traditional beliefs about math teaching and learning and often moves us outside our comfort zone. In order to truly embrace these changes, we must rethink elementary math programs, challenge our old beliefs, confront practices that no longer meet our vision, and reimagine how best to teach math to our elementary students. As leaders, we must first acquaint ourselves with the changes to be sure we are well aware of our vision and the ways in which we can help teachers, students, and parents get there. Then, we must find ways to lead the change within our schools and districts.

Thinking Through the Change

A first step in leading the change is to know where we are in the change process. To do this, we reflect on our program decisions (Chapter 1), observe teaching within our building (Chapter 2), and analyze testing data and student work (Chapter 3). Once we have determined the needs of our students and teachers, we can begin to make program adjustments (Chapter 1), orchestrate professional learning for our teachers (Chapter 4), and communicate with parents to invite them to partner with us in the change process (Chapter 5). Here are some questions to consider as you reflect on where your school or district is in the change process:

DO ALL TEACHERS UNDERSTAND THE TARGET?

- Do teachers understand the need for change? Do they have a clear vison of what we want to see in elementary math classrooms?
- Does it appear that teachers understand the math content and standards they are teaching? Do they know how to address them, or do they need support in this area?
- Do our teachers understand what it looks like to meet or exceed the expectations set by today's math standards?
- Do teachers understand the progression of standards related to math topics?
- Do teachers understand both the content and practice standards and know how to integrate them in their teaching?
- What professional learning opportunities should be arranged in order to support teachers' knowledge related to math content and standards?

HOW IS MATH BEING TAUGHT IN OUR CLASSROOMS?

- In what ways is math talk being used to build understanding? Are teachers asking deep questions, expecting students to explain and justify their thinking, and promoting classroom discourse?
- Is the use of representations an integral component of math teaching and learning? Are students expected to show math ideas in varied ways?
- Is problem solving integrated into all math content teaching? Are students taught to comprehend and solve problems?
- Do teachers make connections between math concepts or between math and the real world? Do teachers connect current skills and concepts to previously taught ones?
- Are students asked to reason about math, observe patterns, and develop insights and generalizations?
- Is formative assessment a regular part of the teaching process? Do teachers use assessment data to modify their teaching?
- How do we monitor the teaching and learning in classrooms in order to provide ongoing support to teachers?
- What professional learning opportunities will be needed to address effective instructional strategies?

- Does instruction balance conceptual understanding, procedural understanding, and application of mathematics skills and concepts?

HOW ARE TEACHERS ADDRESSING INSTRUCTION FOR ALL STUDENTS?

- Are teachers providing interventions for students who are not succeeding?
- Do all students have opportunities with and access to high-quality mathematics tasks?
- Are teachers adjusting instruction when groups of students are not performing well?
- How are teachers using formative assessments to help them identify areas of need, plan interventions for low-performing students, or adjust their instruction?
- Are teachers identifying students who are ready to be challenged with more complex tasks?
- Are teachers given opportunities to discuss specific students who may be struggling with math skills or need to be challenged with more complex skills? Are they given support to know how to address their needs?

IS THERE A POSITIVE DISPOSITION ABOUT MATH AMONG TEACHERS AND STUDENTS?

- Do teachers like teaching math and talk positively about teaching math? If not, how might we support them?
- Do students talk positively about math and believe they can succeed at math? If not, what can be done to change that?
- Is there energy and enthusiasm in our math classrooms? Are students smiling, inquisitive, confident, and engaged? If not, what can we do to change that?
- Do our parents support our math initiatives and feel positive about what we are giving their children? If not, how will we help them understand our vision and our strategies?
- Do our teachers hold high expectations for our students? Do our teachers believe that all students can be successful with mathematics?

IS OUR MATH PROGRAM DESIGNED FOR SUCCESS?

- Is our curriculum aligned with our vision? If not, how might it be adjusted?
- Is our school schedule supportive of our math priorities? If not, how might it be adjusted?
- Does our staff work together to ensure math success for our students (e.g., co-teaching, ongoing communication among teachers)?
- Does our school have the resources to effectively achieve our vision?
- Are we objectively looking at our students' achievement and identifying a plan to address it? Do our teachers know how to effectively analyze data to determine students' needs and to identify teaching modifications?
- What strategies does the staff propose to raise student performance? Do the strategies address the identified needs? Are they doable?
- How will teachers know if the strategies have positively impacted student performance? What data will be collected? When will it be collected? How will it be analyzed?

Making the Change

The change we are talking about is comprehensive. In order to successfully make that change we need to address it with coordinated actions from varied perspectives rather than the piecemeal attempts that have been tried in the past. *Math in Practice* is a comprehensive tool to support your steps toward change. It is designed to give you and your teachers the resources, theory, and practical ideas that allow that change to happen. This series provides

- a rationale for changing math teaching and discussions of instructional strategies that get us there (*Guide for Teachers*)
- content discussions to help teachers better understand the math they are teaching, including the skill progression from the year prior to the following year (About the Math section of the grade-level books)
- a wealth of teaching ideas and lesson ideas specific to the grade-level content (grade-level books)

- reflective lessons that show the decisions that effective teachers make in the planning, delivery, and assessment of grade-level lessons (the "Thinking Through a Lesson" feature in the grade-level books)
- videos to show math teaching in action (online resources)
- resources like recording sheets, math tools, and assessment activities to make lesson planning easier (online resources)
- questions to guide faculty study groups (*Guide for Teachers*)
- tools for planning and conducting professional development (*Guide for Administrators* and online resources).

Let's do this! Let's build a cadre of elementary math teachers who know math content and standards, are willing to try new strategies, and like math and want to ignite excitement within their students. Let's fill our schools with students who understand math concepts, can perform math procedures, can think like problem solvers, can talk about their math reasoning, and can observe, conjecture, and generalize about math ideas. Let's build school districts in which math is a priority, with programs, resources, and professional learning opportunities that support that priority. Let's build a community of parents that recognizes that there were many limitations to traditional ways of thinking about math and teaching math, and who embrace new strategies in an effort to give more to their children than what was given to them. And, most importantly, let's create an elementary math community in which all stakeholders let go of their fear of math, anxiety about math, or dislike of math, but instead discover that math is intriguing, practical, sensible, and fun! The change starts with us. Let's get started!

References and Additional Resources

References

Dweck, Carol. 2007. *Mindset: The New Psychology of Success*. New York: Ballantine Books.

Manouchehri, Azita, and Terry Goodman. 2000. "Implementing Mathematics Reform: The Challenge Within." *Educational Students in Mathematics* 42, no. 1: 1–34.

National Council of Supervisors of Mathematics. 2014. *It's Time: Themes and Imperatives for Mathematics Education*. Bloomington, IN: Solution Tree Press.

National Council of Teachers of Mathematics. 1991. *Professional Standards for Teaching Mathematics*. Reston, VA: NCTM.

————. 2000. *Principles and Standards for School Mathematics*. Reston, VA: NCTM.

————. 2014. *Principles to Actions: Ensuring Mathematical Success for All*. Reston, VA: NCTM.

————. *The Role of the Elementary Mathematics Specialists in the Teaching and Learning of Mathematics*, position statement. http://www.nctm.org/Standards-and-Positions/Position-Statements/The-Role-of-Elementary-Mathematics-Specialists-in-the-Teaching-and-Learning-of-Mathematics/.

National Governors Association Center for Best Practices and Council of Chief State School Officers. 2010. *Common Core State Standards for Mathematics*. Accessed on December 9, 2015. www.corestandards.org/assets/CCSSI_Math%20Standards.pdf.

National Research Council. 2001. *Adding It Up: Helping Children Learn Mathematics*. Washington, DC: National Academy Press.

Olson, Jo, and Jeffrey Barrett. 2004. "Coaching Teachers to Implement Mathematics Reform Recommendations." *Mathematics Teacher Education and Development* 6: 63–78.

U.S. Department of Education. 2009. *Assisting Students Struggling with Mathematics: Response to Intervention (RtI) for Elementary and Middle Schools*. http://ies.ed.gov/ncee/wwc/pdf/practice_guides/rti_math_pg_042109.pdf.

Additional Resources

Boaler, Jo. 2015. *What's Math Got to Do with It?* New York: Penguin Books.

Coates, Grace Davila, and Jean Kerr Stenmark. 1997. *Family Math for Young Children*. Berkeley, CA: Regents of the University of California.

Coates, Grace Davila, and Virginia Thompson. 2003. *Family Math II: Achieving Success in Mathematics*. Berkeley, CA: Regents of the University of California.

Danielson, Christopher. 2015. *Common Core Math for Parents for Dummies*. Hoboken, NJ: John Wiley & Sons.

Stenmark, Jean Kerr, Virginia Thompson, and Ruth Cossey. 1986. *Family Math*. Berkeley, CA: Regents of the University of California.

Whitenack, Joy, Laurie O. Cavey, and Catherine Henney. 2015. *It's Elementary: A Parent's Guide to K–5 Mathematics*. Reston, VA: National Council of Teachers of Mathematics.

The Elementary Math Specialists and Teacher Leaders Project: http://www.mathspecialists.org.

The Math Forum Internet Library on Tracking: http://mathforum.org/library/ed_topics/tracking/.

Online Resources

To access the online resources, visit http://hein.pub/MathinPractice.
Enter your email address and password (or click "Create a New
Account" to set up an account). Once you have logged in, enter
keycode MIPGA and click "Register".

Chapter 1

Coaching Job Descriptions

Sample School Schedules

Chapter 2

Observing Math Standards

Observing Math Teachers

Chapter 3

Contributing Factors Recording Sheet

Data Action Plan

Constructed Response Assessments
    for Kindergarten

Constructed Response Assessments
    for Grade 1

Constructed Response Assessments
    for Grade 2

Constructed Response Assessments
    for Grade 3

Constructed Response Assessments
    for Grade 4

Constructed Response Assessments
    for Grade 5

Analyzing Student Work to
    Guide Instruction

Implications for Instruction

Chapter 4

Teacher Needs Assessment

Sample Collaborative Planning Agenda

Sample Book Study Agenda

Goals and Commitments for a Book Study

Book Study Reflection Sheets

Workshop Planning Notes

Sample PD Agenda

Professional Development Feedback Forms

Teacher to Teacher Feedback

Observing Teaching from a Video Clip

Chapter 5

Family Math Night

Math Fair Projects

Kindergarten Math Month Calendar

Grade 1 Math Month Calendar

Grade 2 Math Month Calendar

Grade 3 Math Month Calendar

Grade 4 Math Month Calendar

Grade 5 Math Month Calendar